STAR WARS™

THE EMPIRE STRIKES BACK

It was the summer of 1977–the summer of *Star Wars*–and George Lucas was already at work on a new story. Only this time, it wasn't just for one film, but for what would become the next two episodes of the original *Star Wars* trilogy.

The Empire Strikes Back came out in May 1980 and it became immediately apparent that this wasn't just another sequel, but a space-fantasy masterpiece and–like the first film–a modern fairy tale for all ages. To many fans, it was not only one of the most important chapters in the Skywalker saga–it was their favorite *Star Wars* movie.

Through on-set interviews with the cast and crew, fun facts, production photos, and original concept art, this official Special delves deep into the story of Luke Skywalker and Darth Vader, Leia Organa and Han Solo, the droids, and Hoth, the ice planet. Relive the challenges of filming in Norway, the creation of the swamp planet Dagobah, and discover the secrets behind the development of iconic characters Lando Calrissian, Boba Fett, and Jedi Master Yoda…

TITAN EDITORIAL
Editor Jonathan Wilkins
Managing Editor Martin Eden
Art Director Oz Browne
Senior Designer Andrew Leung
Assistant Editor Phoebe Hedges
Production Controller Caterina Falqui
Senior Production Controller Jackie Flook
Sales and Circulation Manager Steve Tothill
Direct Marketing Assistant George Wickenden
Marketing and Advertisement Assistant Lauren Noding
Publicist Imogen Harris
Acquisitions Editor Duncan Baizley
Publishing Director Ricky Claydon
Publishing Director John Dziewiatkowski
Operations Director Leigh Baulch
Publishers Nick Landau & Vivian Cheung

DISTRIBUTION
U.S. Newsstand: Total Publisher Services, Inc.
John Dziewiatkowski, 630-851-7683
U.S. Distribution: Ingrams Periodicals,
Curtis Circulation Company
U.K. Newsstand: Marketforce, 0203 787 9199
U.S./U.K. Direct Sales Market: Diamond Comic Distributors
For more info on advertising contact adinfo@titanemail.com

Contents © 2021 Lucasfilm Ltd. & TM. All Rights Reserved

First edition: June 2021

Star Wars: The Empire Strikes Back 40th Anniversary Special Edition is published by Titan Magazines, a division of Titan Publishing Group Limited, 144 Southwark Street, London SE1 0UP

Printed in the U.S.

For sale in the U.S., Canada, U.K., and Eire

ISBN: 9781787734234
Titan Authorized User. TMN 13736

No part of this publication may be reproduced, stored in a retrival system, or transmitted, in any form or by any means, without the prior written permission of the publisher. A CIP catalogue record for this title is available from the British Library.

10 9 8 7 6 5 4 3 2 1

LUCASFILM EDITORIAL
Senior Editor Brett Rector
Art Director Troy Alders
Creative Director Michael Siglain
Story Group Leland Chee, Pablo Hidalgo, Matt Martin
Creative Art Manager Phil Szostak
Asset Management Chris Argyropoulos, Nicole LaCoursiere, Sarah Williams
Special Thanks: Lynne Hale, Christopher Troise, Eugene Paraszczuk

DISNEY PUBLISHING WORLDWIDE
GLOBAL MAGAZINES, COMICS AND PARTWORKS

Publisher Lynn Waggoner Editorial Director Bianca Coletti Editorial Team Guido Frazzini (Director, Comics), Stefano Ambrosio (Executive Editor, New IP), Carlotta Quattrocolo (Executive Editor, Franchise), Camilla Vedove (Senior Manager, Editorial Development), Behnoosh Khalili (Senior Editor), Julie Dorris (Senior Editor) Design Enrico Soave (Senior Designer) Art Ken Shue (VP, Global Art), Roberto Santillo (Creative Director), Marco Ghiglione (Creative Manager), Manny Mederos (Creative Manager), Stefano Attardi (Computer Art Designer) Portfolio Management Olivia Ciancarelli (Director) Business & Marketing Mariantonietta Galla (Senior Manager, Franchise), Virpi Korhonen (Editorial Manager) Text Alessandro Ferrari, Marco Rizzo, Steve Behling, Silvia Dell'Amore Graphic Design co-d S.r.l. – Milano Pre-Press co-d S.r.l. – Milano, Lito milano srl

CONTENTS

⊥ΞVI VΙᏑ∩17VΙ ⊃∿⊥71⊃VΙ∿ ƎΚ⅃⊃

THE MYTH GROWS...

n May 1977, George Lucas' gamble paid off. *Star Wars*: A film different from all others had just been released, yet it was also a film influenced by genres and themes that audiences were familiar and comfortable with, and it had proved to be a huge success. To droves of filmgoers throughout the world it offered a distinctive new take on sci-fi, a blend of western and fantasy, featuring memorable characters and breathtaking special effects. Now Lucas was not only hoping to repeat his earlier success, but to improve upon it and expand his mythic story of good versus evil. The very first *Star Wars* would go down in history as *Star Wars: A New Hope*, and in the wake of that success, work was about to begin on a sequel, *Star Wars:* Episode V *The Empire Strikes Back*. There remained lots of questions to answer. What would be the fate of Luke Skywalker? Would he become a Jedi Knight like his father? Would Han Solo ever really abandon the Rebel Alliance? Would Princess Leia and the Rebel Alliance go on to defeat the Empire?

With the first *Star Wars* film fans had only gotten a brief glimpse of a complex galaxy, as complex as the making of the sequel would turn out to be. Expectations were high, the script was ambitious, the budget grew by leaps and bounds, day after day as production went on. As far as Lucas was concerned, he had every intention of maintaining control over his creations, to the point of financing what would be another colossal blockbuster himself. This is the story of Luke, Han, Leia... and new friends like Yoda, new enemies like Boba Fett, and ambiguous co-protagonists like Lando Calrissian. This is the story of *The Empire Strikes Back*, perhaps the most beloved film in the saga, by fans and critics alike.

The 1979 theatrical advance one-sheet, or teaser poster (left), for *The Empire Strikes Back*, designed by Tony Seiniger and David Reneric, who also developed the approved crew-gear logo (right).

The Empire Strikes Back By Numbers

8 Number of R2-D2 droids used in the film

64 Number of sets built for the film

65 feet Diameter of the full-sized *Millennium Falcon* set

124 minutes Running time

126 Theaters on opening

180 days Duration of principal photography

$4,910,483 Opening weekend box office gross

$547,879,454 Worldwide Box Office Gross

A Partial List of Costs

Rental of an elephant to model locomotion for the walkers: $3,467

Small *Millennium Falcon* model: $10,000

Boba Fett's *Slave I* model: $15,000

Darth Vader's *Executor* ship model: $42,000

Star Destroyer 10-foot model: $55,000

Lawrence Kasdan's fee for rewriting and polishing the script: $60,000

AT-ST walker model: $80,000 to $100,000

Harrison Ford's fee: $100,000

Soundtrack, performed by the London Symphony Orchestra: $250,000

Set construction: $3,500,000

Initial budget: $18,000,000

Final cost: $30,478,433

A NEW HOPE RECAP

Blending elements from the fantastic imaginary he had grown up with, a promising young director, George Lucas, came up with the idea for a long, complex saga somewhere between fantasy and science-fiction. Released as a self-contained film with an evocative title, *Star Wars* would soon become a pop-culture phenomenon and a huge box-office hit, which paved the way for George Lucas to follow suit and let the legend unfold. The story Lucas had come up with, rife with knights, princesses, pirates and an evil despot, slaked worldwide audiences' thirst for adventure. But evidently they still wanted more.

he galaxy quakes with fear when the Galactic Empire builds an enormous, seemingly unstoppable weapon, the Death Star. The Rebel Alliance manages to get its hands on the Death Star plans, which are in the safekeeping of Princess Leia of the planet Alderaan. But her starship is captured by an Imperial Star Destroyer under the command of Darth Vader, fearsome and powerful emissary of the Galactic Empire, and overrun by an army of stormtroopers. Vader takes the princess hostage, but not before Leia manages to place a message—and the Death Star plans—inside an astromech droid, R2-D2. He and his sidekick C-3PO hightail it in an escape pod and wind up on the desert planet Tatooine.

The two droids are captured by Jawa traders and sold to Luke Skywalker, a young and ambitious moisture farmer who lives with his aunt and uncle. While cleaning R2-D2, Luke accidentally sets off Princess Leia's message and hears her say the name, "Obi-Wan Kenobi". While Luke had never heard that exact name, he figured it must be a relative of the old hermit, Ben Kenobi, who lived out beyond the Dune Sea. That night, R2-D2 sets out on his own to find "Old" Ben, and it isn't until morning that Luke and C-3PO are able to catch up to him. The three are attacked

01

01 R2-D2 reveals
   Princess Leia's
   all-important
   message.

02 Han Solo and his
   co-pilot Chewbacca
   take control of the
   Millennium Falcon.

03 Luke Skywalker,
   Princess Leia, and
   Han Solo prepare to
   face the enemy.

04

by Tusken Raiders, and then saved by Ben, who mimics the wail of a krayt dragon. Inside his cottage, Ben reveals that he is Obi-Wan Kenobi, a Jedi Knight who served the Galactic Republic before the rise of the Empire. He also reveals to Luke that his father was a Jedi Knight as well, and gives Luke the lightsaber that had once belonged to him. Luke asks how his father died, and Obi-Wan tells him about a former pupil, Darth Vader, who had been lured to the dark side of the Force—Darth Vader killed Luke's father. In the process, Luke learns about a mystical energy field known as the Force that gives the Jedi Knights their power.

In the presence of Obi-Wan, R2-D2 delivers the message sent to him by Princess Leia, who begs him to deliver the droid (which contains information vital to the survival of the Rebel Alliance) safely to her father on

Alderaan. Ben asks Luke to come with him, but Luke declines, though he offers to take Kenobi to the nearest port. On the way, they discover the smoldering frame of a sandcrawler, owned by the same Jawas who sold his uncle R2-D2 and C-3PO. Kenobi knows who is responsible— Imperial stormtroopers. Despite Ben's pleas, Luke heads home, only to discover both his aunt and uncle have been murdered by stormtroopers looking for the droids.

Left with no choice, Luke teams up with Obi-Wan, R2-D2 and C-3PO, and the group head to Mos Eisley, specifically the cantina, hoping to find a pilot who can fly them to Alderaan. There, they meet smuggler Han Solo and his Wookiee copilot, Chewbacca. Han agrees to take our friends to Alderaan on his *Millennium Falcon*—for a hefty sum. The fee will offset the debt Han owes to mobster Jabba the Hutt. But before

05

Han can leave the cantina, one of Jabba's thugs, Greedo, asks him for the money he owes. Han doesn't have it yet, and Greedo suggests Jabba might settle in exchange for Han's ship. A lethal exchange follows, leaving Han the sole survivor.

Meanwhile, Leia is tortured on the Death Star by Darth Vader and the battle station's commander, Grand Moff Tarkin. Her resolve is so strong that she reveals nothing to her captors. In order to force Leia to reveal the location of the hidden rebel base, Tarkin threatens to use the Death Star to destroy Alderaan. Leia hopes that giving Tarkin the location of an abandoned rebel base might spare her homeworld from destruction, but Tarkin orders his men to fire regardless.

En route to Alderaan aboard the *Falcon*, Luke begins training under Obi-Wan. Upon reaching the location where Alderaan should be, all they

06

find is a cluster of asteroids. Soon the freighter is captured and pulled on board the Death Star. The group quickly learns that Princess Leia herself is imprisoned within the space station. While Obi-Wan deactivates the tractor beam that's keeping the *Falcon* from leaving, Luke and Han, disguised as stormtroopers,

and Chewie, their phoney prisoner, succeed in freeing Princess Leia. But before they can make it back to the ship, Obi-Wan encounters Darth Vader. The two duel it out with their lightsabers. Once sure that his friends can escape, Obi-Wan allows Darth Vader to kill him. The group boards the *Falcon* and takes off, unaware that a tracking device has been planted on the ship.

Arriving at the secret base on Yavin 4, rebel technicians are at last able to analyze the Death Star plans. The rebels spot a weak point and devise a plan of attack. By now the Death Star approaches Yavin 4. Han opts out of the imminent battle, while Luke joins the fleet of rebel starfighters who'll lead the attack on the Death Star. As Luke hones in on the battle station's tiny exhaust port, he is fired upon by Darth Vader, who is leading a squadron of TIE fighters. Luckily Han and Chewie unexpectedly return in the *Falcon* and stave off Darth Vader's attack. Just as Luke is about to fire at the Death Star, he hears Obi-Wan's voice exhorting him to "use the Force." The Death Star is destroyed, and the explosion sends Darth Vader's ship careening through space. On Yavin 4, Luke, Han and Chewbacca are met by Leia, and celebrated as rebel heroes. ☻

04 Darth Vader versus Obi-Wan Kenobi—in a fateful duel.

05 Luke Skywalker, whose life is turned upside-down in *A New Hope*.

06 The rebels attack the Death Star during the climax of *A New Hope*.

⊥ᕮVᑊᐸI⊏⊔ᒪ7∨I ᕐᘝ⊃7ᒪᗡ∨Iᕐᘝ ᕮᏋᑊ⊐

THE EMPIRE STRIKES BACK

Like many other great stories, *The Empire Strikes Back* is based on a three-act structure. Despite the fact that it is the second film in a trilogy, the screenplay—which experienced a troubled production—is exquisitely satisfying even on its own. Science-fiction author and screenwriter Leigh Brackett began work on the script, which, following her death in 1978, was completed by Lawrence Kasdan, based on an outline by George Lucas.

ACT ONE

In which the characters are presented, the context is defined, interpersonal relations are explored and a change in the status quo gets the ball rolling.

A long time ago, in a galaxy far, far away....

Three years after the destruction of the Death Star, members of the Rebel Alliance headed by Princess Leia Organa, fleeing the forces of the Empire, find refuge on the ice planet Hoth. Luke, by this time a point man for the Rebel Alliance, is patrolling the surrounding area. He sees what looks like a meteorite and radios this intelligence to Han. Before he can investigate, Luke is knocked out by a giant wampa. Back at Echo Base, Han informs Leia that he aims to leave soon, so he can make good on his debt to Jabba the Hutt. Leia protests, saying that Han is a natural leader. But he believes the reason Leia doesn't want him to leave is because of her feelings for him.

Realizing Luke has not returned, Han sets out in search of the young rebel. Inside the wampa's cave, a captured Luke uses the Force to escape. He encounters the Force ghost of his mentor, Obi-Wan Kenobi, who urges him to continue training with Jedi Master Yoda on the planet of Dagobah. Han saves Luke, and the two are rescued by rebel pilots. Not long thereafter, an Imperial probe droid picks up signs of life on Hoth. Darth Vader is adamant that the rebels are hiding there, and gives the order to attack.

The Empire arrives on Hoth, and begin their assault on the rebels' base, aided by their monstrous AT-AT walkers.

Despite their dogged resistance, the Rebel Alliance is forced to evacuate.

ACT TWO

In which the hero sets out on a quest, the characters' interpersonal relation-ships mature, and the situation grows worse.

Leia, Han, Chewie, and C-3PO escape aboard the *Millennium Falcon*, but damage to its hyperdrive system slows them down. To dodge Imperial TIE fighters, Han steers his ship into an asteroid field. In the meantime, Darth Vader has summoned bounty hunters to track down his enemies.

Meanwhile, Luke evacuates Hoth aboard his X-wing, where he and R2-D2 set course for Dagobah. After crash landing in a swamp, the pair set up camp, where they are soon greeted by

a tiny creature, who turns out to be Jedi Master Yoda.

Aboard the *Falcon*, Leia and Han share their first kiss. On Dagobah, Yoda teaches Luke the ways of the Force, while warning the young apprentice of the dark side. Luke has a premonition that his friends are in serious trouble. Against the wishes of Yoda and the Force spirit of Obi-Wan, he abandons his training for the time being to come to their aid. The *Falcon* is now headed for Cloud City, the metropolis that floats above the gas giant Bespin, where they are greeted by the smiling Lando Calrissian, an old friend of Han's who might be able to help them. But instead of helping, Lando turns Han and company over to Darth Vader.

ACT THREE
In which the hero and his comrades take on the antagonist. Things change radically after the fight.

Faced with the choice of collaborating with the Empire or having Cloud City destroyed, Lando has betrayed the escaping Rebels. Darth Vader tortures Han and Leia in order to attract Luke's attention and lure him there. He plans to use a carbon-freezing chamber to place Luke in a state of hibernation, before turning him over to his own superior, the fearsome Emperor. But first, Vader uses Han as a test subject, to ensure the process won't kill his prize. Right before he's to be frozen, Leia tells Han she loves him. His reply? "I know." The two kiss, then Han is placed in the chamber. The experiment is a success, and Han is turned over to bounty hunter Boba Fett, who will take him to Jabba the Hutt.

By now, Luke has arrived on Cloud City, and is making his way through the facility to locate his friends. Lando, now realizing the grave error he's made in aiding the Empire, frees Leia, Chewbacca, and C-3PO. They attempt to catch Boba Fett, but they are too late.

Luke and Darth Vader engage in lightsaber combat, and in the process, Luke loses his right hand. Darth Vader tries to lure the young rebel over to the dark side, but Luke resists. He believes that it was Darth Vader who killed his father. Luke is stunned when Vader claims that he, in fact, is Luke's father. Vader urges Luke to join him, so they can rule the galaxy as father and son. But Luke denies his father his victory, throwing himself off a platform into an abyss. Plunging down a huge conduit, Luke nearly falls from Cloud City. Through the Force, he contacts Leia, who is fleeing aboard the *Falcon* with Chewie, Lando and the droids. They turn back and rescue Luke, only to be followed by TIE fighters. R2-D2 at last succeeds in activating the *Falcon*'s hyperdrive, allowing them to elude their pursuers. Leia and Luke reconnect with the Rebel Alliance fleet, where Luke is fitted with a cybernetic hand. He and Leia say goodbye to Lando and Chewbacca, who head to Tatooine in search of Han. ✪

02

03

01 Luke Skywalker—
and his tauntaun—on
the remote ice world of
Hoth. (Previous spread)

02 Danger on the
horizon—in the form of
the AT-ATs.

03 Meeting the
master—Luke
and Yoda.

04 Han Solo's frosty
fate, as Darth Vader
carbon-freezes him.

04

05

05 C-3PO, R2-D2,
Leia, and Luke watch
the *Millennium Falcon*
set off in the search for
Han Solo at the
conclusion of *The
Empire Strikes Back*.

ꓘ ꟾꓥꓩꓷ ꓥꟾꓥꓷꓶ

THE SAGA BEGINS

It was August 1977, and about two months after its premiere *Star Wars* was still number one at the box office. Lucasfilm was beginning negotiations with Fox for the sequel, with the aim to get back the rights to the characters and limit the company's creative control over the filmmaking process. The agreement would be signed at the end of September, giving George Lucas the final cut of the film and offering his company a better profit sharing deal. Meanwhile, trying to rebuild Industrial Light & Magic—which closed down upon the release of the first film—Lucas was hiring back essential collaborators such as artist Ralph McQuarrie and director of visual effects photography Dennis Muren, among others. Everything was ready, but what was the story they would tell?

THE CONCEPT – *Star Wars: Chapter II*, as it was being called at that time, wasn't just a sequel, it was part of a whole saga. The success of *Star Wars*, which an early note written by George Lucas initially placed as Episode VI, was giving its creator the chance to tell it all. In Summer 1977, these were the key elements of the new story: A lost sister trained as a Jedi—a plot that would only find its conclusion in 2019, in *The Rise of Skywalker*, but that would define the main storyline of *The Empire Strikes Back* and *Return of the Jedi* (1983); the

Emperor/Empire that had to be destroyed; the Republic that had to be restored. Also, Lucas returned to an idea abandoned before the first film was shot, an idea that the death of Obi-Wan Kenobi made necessary: Luke needed a new master. "A repulsive, threatening figure can magically change into a most helpful friend." reads one of Lucas' notes on yellow legal-lined pads.

"Talks to trees—shadows move and disappear. He [teacher] was Mynoc. Human-computer. (Vader?) Swordmasters." Two other elements were already present. Obi-Wan's manifestation as a Force spirit and the relationship between Luke and his father,

whose identity was still uncertain: "Somewhere the good father (Ben) watches over the child's fate, ready to assert his power when critically needed. Father changes into Darth Vader, who is a passing manifestation, and will return triumphant. Luke travels to the end of the world and makes sacrifice to undo the spell put on his father. He succeeds and happiness is restored."

One of the events Lucas had to include had nothing to do with his plans for the saga. In January 1977, Mark Hamill (the actor who played Luke Skywalker in *Star Wars*) had a car accident and fractured his nose and cheekbone. His face looked different;

01 Chewbacca
(Peter Mayhew),
Han Solo (Harrison
Ford), Princess Leia
(Carrie Fisher),
Luke Skywalker
(Mark Hamill)
inside the Hoth
rebel base set.

02

therefore, Luke's face had to look different: Chapter II would start with the protagonist being injured. According to Hamill, when he asked Lucas what he would have done if his main actor would have been killed in the car accident, Lucas replied that no one would have replaced him: "There'd be a script change that would have found a long-lost brother or sister, something genetic, so that the Force would be with them."

Later that year, after visual effects artist Joe Johnston was hired back and started working on a snow battle he didn't know much about, Lucas defined other vital elements of the story: "Streamline beginning—Leia to Vader to Luke. Streamline attack plot... Han thinks about Leia.

02 The cockpit of the *Millennium Falcon* was built larger than the one used in *Star Wars*, but Lucas thought it should have been like the original to better simulate the cockpit of bombers.

03 Mark Hamill reprised the role of Luke Skywalker, for which he had trained as an acrobat and a gymnast.

04 Severely injured by a wampa on the ice planet of Hoth, Luke is saved by Han Solo and later put inside a bacta tank to heal. To shoot the scene, Mark Hamill had to learn underwater diving in a short time.

Leia about Han... Threepio blown apart, transported in pieces to area where he can be reassembled. Han Solo, go on mission and never come back. End with Luke thinking about him... Luke develops Force, becomes powerful knight... Luke–R-2 worried about where going; Han and Leia find asteroid field... Luke falls into trap—Vader gets upper hand; Luke barely escapes. On new base... Act I: Love story; into large threat (Emperor)." Every main scene of the story was there, ready to be transposed into a script. But Lucas didn't want to do it himself, for writing *Star Wars* had been the part he enjoyed the least. This time, he planned to hire screenwriters, collaborate with them, give them ideas, and make sure they wouldn't lose sight of the most

important thing: Like the first one, this new film had to be a modern fairy tale for children, with a strong sense of morality and justice. As his notes read: "Reassures, gives hope for the future, and holds out the promise of a happy ending... Discover identity and calling... Intimate that a rewarding, good life is within one's reach despite adversity—but only if one does not shy away from the hazardous struggles without which one can never achieve true identity."

THE WRITERS – In November 1977, Lucas thought he had found his writer: Leigh Brackett, a celebrated author of detective and science-fiction stories, who wrote the script for Howard Hawks' *The Big Sleep* (1946, together with William Faulkner

03

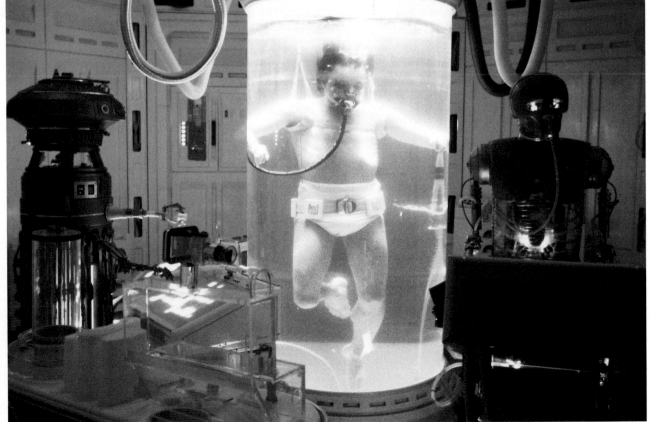

04

05

05 Special effects photography supervisor Richard Edlund shows director Irvin Kershner the optical printer. It was used at the end of the film to put together all the different elements filmed separately and to add visual effects.

06 Visual effects art director Joe Johnston (on the left) and director Irvin Kershner (on the right) in front of a wall of storyboards at Industrial Light & Magic's new home in San Rafael, California.

07 Optical printer operator Kenneth Smith behind the optical printer: designed for *The Empire Strikes Back*, it had two pairs of projectors through which the films would be run, and a camera to rephotograph them.

and Jules Furthman), and later for several John Wayne pictures such as *Rio Bravo* (1959), *Hatari!* (1962), *El Dorado* (1966), and *Rio Lobo* (1970). A fan of those films, Lucas started developing his ideas with Brackett, and on February 21, 1978, she delivered the first draft. Despite following closely Lucas' notes and treatment, starting from the Ice Planet and taking Luke to the bog planet where an alien trained him, the script didn't have the right feeling. The characters didn't sound like the *Star Wars* characters the audience knew and loved. "The truth of it is, I got captivated by the thing; it's in me now," Lucas later commented. "And I can't help but get upset or excited when something isn't the way it's supposed to be. I can see

that world. I know the way the characters live and breathe. In a way, they have taken over. It's the hardest thing in writing to be able to develop individual characters that aren't a reflection of the mind that created them. My thoughts during the story conference weren't fully formed, and I felt her script went off in a completely different direction." George Lucas edited the script, then tried to get in contact with the writer to talk to her, but he found out she had been hospitalized. Leigh Brackett died of cancer on Saturday, March 18, at the age of 60. Without her, Lucas had no choice but to write the second draft himself, while Joe Johnston was already working on the storyboards for the snow battle. In this new version, the story starts

with the epic battle on the ice planet of Hoth, then focuses on smaller conflicts that show the characters' emotional development—such as Luke's training with Yoda, the identity of his father, Han and Leia betrayed by Lando, and Lando's redemption. This structure would be reversed in the next film, which starts with more personal stories and ends with the final battle between the Rebel Alliance and the Empire. Lucas wrote this second draft by hand and made corrections as it was typed up, one of which was about the film's position within the saga. *Star Wars: Chapter II* became *Episode V: The Empire Strikes Back* for the first time.

For the following version of the script, a new writer was hired in June 1978: Lawrence

6

07 Kasdan, who just transformed Lucas' treatment for *Raiders of the Lost Ark* into a script. "The reason George wanted me to write it is because I'm really strong in people," said Kasdan. "That's what all my original screenplays are about. They tend to be much smaller stories about a smaller number of people, comedies and thrillers, but they're still entertainment. George thought it was very important that *Empire* have that. If anything, we wanted *Empire* to have deeper characterization, more complex psychology for the characters than the first *Star Wars*." Knowing that a third film would follow helped Kasdan sort out which ideas to use and which to keep for the sequel. A third draft was completed in early August and a fourth one

08

in October. "It was a constant battle between character and action, between speed and any kind of respite, which I believe in and I like to see in a film," said the writer. At the beginning of 1979, Kasdan was still working on the last minor changes for the fifth and final draft, which would be ready just days before the filming started.

THE DIRECTOR – Between the end of 1977 and the beginning of 1978, Gary Kurtz, vice president of production on *Star Wars*, was looking for a director since George Lucas didn't want to direct the sequel: "If I directed *Empire*, then I'd have to direct the next one and the next for the rest of my life. I've never really liked directing. I became a director because I didn't like directors telling me how to edit,

and I became a writer because I had to write something in order to be able to direct something. So I did everything out of necessity, but what I really like is editing." After talking with Alan Parker (who directed *Bugsy Malone* in 1976), John Badham (who directed *Saturday Night Fever* in 1977), and a few others, Kurtz and Lucas found out it was harder than expected. According to Kurtz, many directors didn't want to be involved in the sequel to a successful picture because the reputation of the first film could overshadow them. Also, the film didn't need just any director, but one who believed in the material, who could develop the *Star Wars* galaxy without forgetting this had to be an adventure story. Lucas realized the right person was Irvin Kershner, who had

taught at the University of Southern California's School of Cinema where Lucas had studied and who appreciated his early works. Kershner was vastly experienced—he started directing in the 1950s—and loved the technical aspects and visual possibilities that *Empire* could offer: "I told George that the only way I'd do the film is if I felt I could top the first one. He laughed and said that's why he wanted me to do it. He said, 'It's not a sequel. This is a continuing saga.'" The negotiation between Lucasfilm and the director lasted from February to April, 26, 1978, the day Irvin Kershner signed his contract. But pre-production had started, and he was already involved in every aspect. The company George Lucas wanted was taking form, and the saga he had in mind was coming to life. ☮

08 On the Bespin landing platform set, Kershner talks with actor Billy Dee Williams (Lando Calrissian) while shooting the arrival of Han Solo (Harrison Ford, in the background) and the *Millennium Falcon*.

09 Director Irvin Kershner on the Echo Base set with actress Carrie Fisher, during a break from shooting. Fisher is wearing her Princess Leia snow outfit.

09

10

10 Harrison Ford (Han Solo) and Mark Hamill (Luke Skywalker) discuss the Hoth medical center scene, in which Leia kisses Luke, who is recovering from the wampa attack, in front of Solo.

‡Ǝⴸ ⴸꞀꞰⴸⵑⴸ

HOTH

With temperatures as low as -60°C during the nights and landscapes constantly buried under ice and snow, this is one of the most inhospitable planets of the galaxy. The almost unlivable climate is caused by Hoth's great distance from the primary sun of the system and also by its wide elliptical orbit—as a result, it takes the planet 526 standard days to round that sun. Intense winds and snowstorms constantly blow the frozen surface of Hoth, shaping the landscape and amplifying the extreme cold. Even droids, speeders, and transports have a tough life here. While Hoth's hostile environment might dissuade visitors and explorers, it makes the planet a very good place to hide, as the Rebellion knows well. But even Hoth isn't remote enough to elude the Empire's probe droids and keep the Echo Base safe.

THE ORIGIN – As he did for *A New Hope*, George Lucas made a list of planets in his notes when he started imagining the sequel. Among them, he named: the Wookiee planet—on which production illustrator Ralph McQuarrie started working since he signed his contract in October 1977, but that would not appear in the film; a gas planet called Hoth—which would later become Bespin where Lando's Cloud City floats; and a generic "Ice Planet". It was only in the second draft of the script in 1978 that the name was assigned to the actual ice planet where the rebels would set up their new outpost. From the Ice Kingdom of Mongo featured in Alex Raymond's *Flash Gordon* comics series (March 12, 1939 to April 7, 1940) to Howard Hawks's *The Thing from Another World* (1951), several influences shaped Hoth's concept and development. This is how Lucas himself described the planet in 1977: "We could start on the Ice Planet, which would be striking. We've never been there before, an underground installation in a giant snow bank. Very hostile, with wind blowing around and the cold."

In parallel to the world of the Wookiees, covered in huge trees, McQuarrie was already painting ice and snow: based on Lucas' instructions, since no finished script was available at that time, the artist

01 Final painting of "Ice Castle" by Ralph McQuarrie, December 7-9, 1977

02 Mark Hamill on the
Hoth location in Finse,
Norway. Because of the
harsh conditions and
frequent snow storms,
many scenes had to be
shot a few feet away
from the hotel, including
the one where Luke
flees from the ice cave.

03 Rebel troopers are forced to retreat during the Imperial attack. To shoot some of the scenes with explosives, the second-unit crew employed mannequins dressed up as rebel soldiers.

was developing Darth Vader's home. Initially set in a cold environment, the metal castle of the Sith Lord was later placed amid boiling lava, but it didn't make it in the film anyway—its first appearance would only be in 2005 in *Revenge of the Sith*, though it was not actually called Vader's castle in the final prequel film. Some of the concept paintings were later converted to first illustrate the rebel base in the context of Hoth. In the following months the metal structure disappeared and the base was moved inside the ice caves, which were considered natural to the planet. Trying to figure out the design of the interiors, Ralph McQuarrie and visual effects art director Joe Johnston imagined how the rebels carved the ice out to make room for the hangar and the equipment: "It was my feeling that lasers would be used to accomplish the cutting in long, straight lines. That helped give me a key to part of the solution."

PROBLEMS ON SET – After several trips across northern Europe, in the spring of 1978 the Norwegian town of Finse was chosen as the location for Hoth. According to associate producer Robert Watts, the glacier in Finse provided "the uninterrupted, treeless expanse" that was ideal for shooting the ice planet scenes. There was also a hotel along the railway line which was thirty minutes away from the glacier, and therefore quite convenient for accommodating the film crew. Yet filming in Finse proved very challenging due to the chilling weather conditions. With temperatures around -30°C (almost like the fictional planet Hoth), violent snowstorms and high winds, the film crew found itself facing Norway's coldest winter in a hundred years.

Basic tasks such as reloading a camera, using a tape recorder

04

or even, as admitted by director Irvin Kershner, going to the bathroom were extremely difficult and required the crew to think on their feet and quickly come up with alternative solutions. One such solution was the decision to shoot some scenes just a few feet away from the hotel: "If the camera would've turned around, you'd have seen a big hotel behind you," said assistant producer Jim Bloom, "but because of the weather, it looked like you were out in the middle of nowhere." Filming started on Monday, March 5, 1979, under quite unfortunate circumstances: a trench that had been dug a few days before by the construction crew was buried in snow, meaning that none of the planned scenes could be shot; trains were unable to reach Finse and the road to the railway line was blocked. The situation was so critical that production decided to call Harrison Ford in a week early to film one of his scenes instead. "We thought we could shoot his sequence that, because of

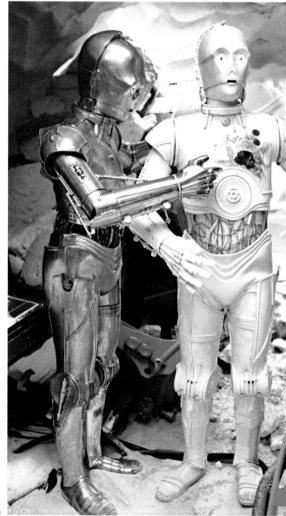

05

04 Ford and Hamill in their snow costumes. Rebel troops wore light-colored uniforms to camouflage with the snow.

05 C-3PO (left) and the unlucky K-3PO (right), who did not survive the Battle of Hoth.

06 Echo Station 3-T-8 rebel scouts in a live-action image, inspired by McQuarrie's painting below.

07 McQuarrie's original painting. Echo Station 3-T-8 rebel scouts were the first ones to detect the Imperial forces.

losing Stage 3 [destroyed by a fire in January 24, while it was housing the hotel lobby of Stanley Kubrick's *The Shining*], we were going to shoot at Leeds Studios 2," said associate producer Robert Watts. "If we could get this sequence successfully in Norway, this would obviate us from having to go out to Leeds." Due to three avalanches that had cut off the railway road, however, Ford's journey wasn't going to be an easy one: in order to successfully reach Finse from Oslo, the actor had to take a train, two taxis and was eventually picked up by a snowplow twenty-three miles from Finse. The last main unit scene was shot on Monday, March 11, whereas the second unit faced further weather variations which led them to run over schedule. "We were supposed to be there for three weeks," said Bloom. "We were there for eight." The unit wrapped on Tuesday, April 3; on the same day, another avalanche took place—a phenomenon which, according to locals, and somewhat frustratingly for the cast, meant the arrival of spring.

08

THE SNOWTROOPERS – As suggested by their name, snowtroopers are Imperial troopers whose armor has been enhanced specifically to endure extreme-cold weather. First seen in *The Empire Strikes Back*, snowtroopers are are the first-ever Imperial soldiers shown to have customized, climate-specific gear. Their suits and backpacks are designed to maintain body warmth, while their masks feature heaters to help them breathe in the cold. Both Ralph McQuarrie and Joe Johnston came up with several costume concepts, but only Johnston's were eventually used for the final design. Whilst McQuarrie's version had a clear

Samurai flair ("It was a little like something worn in Noh dramas", he said, referring to the classical Japanese dance-drama), Johnston envisioned a relatively simple and plain armor design.

Once approved by George Lucas, the finalized design was then passed onto costume designer John Mollo, who was also part of the production team of *A New Hope* and had just finished working on the costumes for Ridley Scott's *Alien*. To stay within budget, Mollo further simplified the armor and cut down the number of snowtrooper costumes from twenty to fifteen. The final version was relatively similar

to the standard stormtrooper; the main differences were the addition of a face cowl made with layers of white PVC Vinyl, an insulated cape, twill pants, ice boots and soft gloves, which were actually adapted from gardening ones! Along with the fifteen snowtroopers, Mollo and his team created a separate armor for the troops' commander, which featured a vacuum-formed shield in lieu of the cowl and additions such as a rank bar, a blaster pistol and holster. To further distinguish the commander, production inverted the shoulder bell orientation and opted for grey moon boots in place of the snow boots worn by the troops.

08 Imperial snowtroopers assault Echo Base on Hoth. Their suit and backpack systems are equipped with long-lasting batteries that made them able to endure extreme temperatures for up to two weeks.

09 Rebel snowspeeders endeavor to slow down relentless Imperial walkers during the Battle of Hoth. In order to successfully operate the mechanical legs, AT-AT pilots had to undergo rigorous training.

AT-AT WALKERS – All Terrain Armored Transport Walkers (more commonly known as AT-ATs) were colossal, four-legged army units used by the Empire to attack the Rebellion's base during the Battle of Hoth. Their impressive height (over 60 feet tall) and slow, relentless movements made AT-ATs an extremely daunting weapon able to intimidate whoever crossed their path. As explained by director of photography Dennis Muren, the AT-AT's concept was influenced by the U.S. military armament deployed in Vietnam. As such, Johnston's early sketches featured tank-like vehicles whose design, however, turned

out to be too "conventional" for an alleged space machine. Further inspiration came from illustrations commissioned to concept artist Syd Mead for U.S. Steel promotional materials: "It was a promotional brochure put out by U.S. Steel in the early 1960s," said Johnston, "and contained a whole slew of full-color paintings indicating, 'What steel will be used for in the future.' Interestingly enough, one of the paintings showed a four-legged walking truck! That's where the initial walker idea came from."

According to Lucas, AT-ATs were ultimately influenced by the spider-like vehicles featured

in H.G Well's novel *The War of the Worlds*. "The walkers were inspired by *War of the Worlds* more than anything else," Lucas said "where the Martians walked in machines like giant spiders. I was trying to come up with a way of making this battle different." To bring AT-ATs to life on screen, Johnston and effects director of photography Dennis Muren persuaded Lucas to use stop-motion, a filmmaking technique in which objects are maneuvered between frames to create the illusion of movement. The animation process entails taking a picture of a static object, moving it in an almost unnoticeable

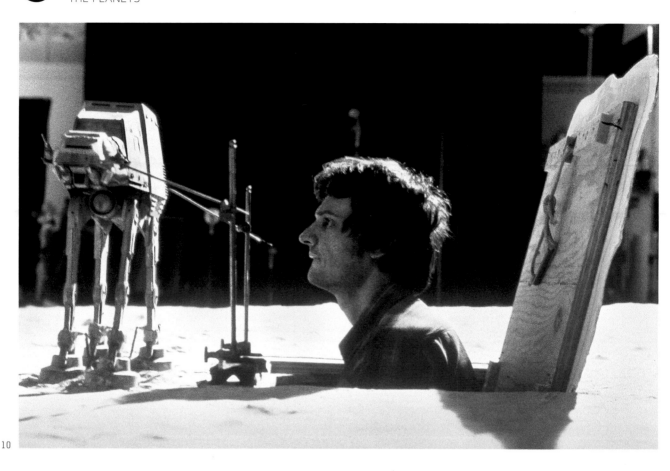

10

manner, and taking another picture. Images are then played back consecutively, making the objects appear as if they are moving on their own. "I'd been a stop-motion animator and cameraman in my past, so I was real familiar with that," explained Muren. "And I just thought we should do at least that chunk of the film with stop-motion, which was a tried-and-true technique that we could schedule and we could get done—and if it looked a little funky, it's okay because they're machines anyway." If Muren and Johnston had a pivotal role in defining how the Imperial walkers would eventually look, animator Jon Berg was crucial in realizing a fully functioning prototype. "If there was one person responsible for getting the walkers on the screen, it was Jon Berg," Johnston would later say. "He developed the entire armature, working from just a

couple of my rough sketches. And he managed to integrate a lot of experimental ideas that worked really well." In order to make a successful prototype, several aspects had to be taken into consideration. In Berg's own words, the model had to be "poseable," that is, capable of holding a specific pose "in each position you place it without slipping or sliding." To achieve credible motion, Berg based the walkers' iconic walk on a real-life elephant that he filmed in early 1979 (the very same elephant, Mardij, had been used for the bantha in *A New Hope*). Overall, preparation for the walker scenes took around 10 months, while a single shot took a whole day to produce, with an average of one second per hour. As commented by stop-motion technician Doug Beswick, "the increments for the walker movements were so small, they could hardly be gauged!"

11

12

3

14

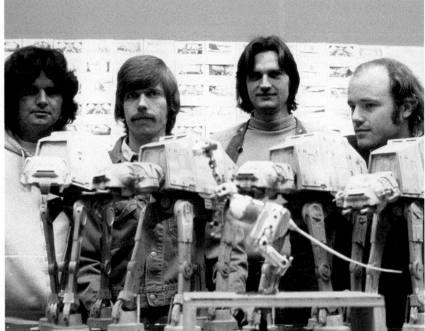

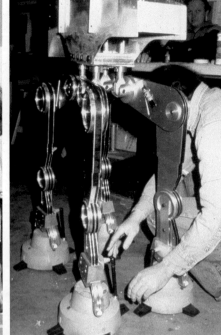

15

10 Stop-motion and special effects artist Jon Berg brings an AT-AT walker to life... frame by frame.

11 Each shot animated in stop-motion would take around 4-6 hours of work to be completed.

12 The pyro model of the AT-AT—oversized to properly scale the fire and smoke—was held up by cables, which detached and made it fall.

13 Stop-motion technicians and animators Tom St. Amand, Doug Beswick, Jon Berg and Phil Tippett with the finalized walkers.

14 A walker prototype developed by Jon Berg and Joe Johnston.

15 An AT-AT walker model on a set, in front of a matte painting of Hoth. To simulate snow, stage technicians employed tiny microballoons to be sprinkled across the miniature.

As for the noises, sound effects recorder Randy Thom researched metal fabricators to find a convincing sound for the vehicles' motion. Eventually, he recorded metal shears, particularly useful for their multisyllabic sound.

"The objective was to give the walkers a real sense of mass and weight," explained sound designer Ben Burtt. "Randy went out and recorded some of those big metallic stamping machines. Then I picked out parts of the recording I liked

and made it into a rhythmic walk cycle." Additionally, Burtt needed a squeaking sound similar to "a knee joint," which he successfully achieved thanks to a dumpster lid that had been left near his house. ✪

16   17

16 Han Solo finds and destroys the Imperial probe droid on Hoth, which ran on tracks concealed in the snow. The rig, together with the use of long shots, made the droid look like as it was floating.

17 The (soon to be called) Viper probe droid arrived at ILM in August 1979. Along with five arms and a blaster, Imperial probe droids included a self-destruct mechanism and repulsorlift engines.

18 Visual effects photographer Richard Edlund poses with a full-scale probe droid and a smaller miniature.

19 Rebel troopers
prepare to fire the
dish laser cannon
during the Imperial
attack on the ice planet
of Hoth. Despite the
Empire's victory over
the Rebel Alliance, Darth
Vader would fail to catch
Luke Skywalker.

20

20 A snowtrooper fires an E-Web heavy repeating blaster, an incredibly powerful Imperial weapon.

21 After the rebel power generators have been destroyed, snowtroopers ruthlessy invade Echo Base.

22 Actor and bodybuilder David Prowse as Dark Lord of the Sith, Darth Vader. According to Prowse, the armor was far from comfortable: indeed, it was made of quilted leather and weighed around 48 pounds.

21

23

24

23 Rebel soldiers carry
equipment and prepare
for the Imperial assault.

24 A painting of Hoth
used as the background
of a miniature set for the
AT-AT stop-motion
animation.

25 DF.9 turret
placement, concept art
by Ralph McQuarrie.

26 "Ice Cave" (reverse
view) by McQuarrie, May
10–11, 1978.

27 "Ice Cave"
(looking toward door)
by McQuarrie. An early
version of the tauntaun
can be spotted in the
background.

28

28 A behind-the-scenes
photo of Mark Hamill
(Luke Skywalker)
manning a laser
ice-cutter at Echo Base.

29 Rebel pilots prepare to leave Hoth aboard the X-wings after the Imperial forces entered the base.

30 Rogue Two pilot Zev Senesca was played by actor Christopher Malcolm.

31 Young pilot Wedge Antilles (played by Denis Lawson) flying as Rogue Three in the battle of Hoth.

32 "Feeling all right, sir?" asks rear gunner Dak Ralter as he (right) and Rogue Leader Luke Skywalker (left) prepare to hold off the Empire.

33 Derek "Hobbie" Klivian (played by Richard Oldfield) serves as Luke's wingman during the Battle of Hoth.

34 Dak Ralter is played by John Morton, who also appeared as Boba Fett.

LIFE ON HOTH

Despite the harsh conditions and scant vegetation, Hoth is home at least to two prominent indigenous species: the tauntaun, a lizard-like animal, and the wampa, a predatory creature at the top of the food chain. To survive on Hoth, both creatures have evolved to withstand the perilous climate: tauntauns rest overnight as the nighttime would be deadly otherwise; wampas have developed a thick fur and only hunt in proximity of their shelters. Whilst tauntauns mainly feed on lichen and can be domesticated, the same definitely does not apply to wampas. These ferocious predators attack by stunning and dragging their prey back to their caves, something that Luke Skywalker learns at his own expense.

THE TAUNTAUN – Regardless of their feral nature, tauntauns proved to be loyal companions of the Rebel Alliance. They are, in fact, often used as mounts by rebels on patrol duties, who prefer them to T-47 airspeeders because of their better resistance to subzero temperatures. The unpleasant smell they exude, however, makes the rebels' ride anything but comfortable. Originally envisioned as a "giant snow lizard" by George Lucas, the tauntaun went through several makeovers and redevelopments. In his early sketches, which date back to December 1977, Ralph McQuarrie depicted the tauntaun as a dinosaur-like creature; after showing the artwork to Lucas, however, it was clear to him that a change of direction was needed. "I thought it was going to be used in the middle of the desert," said McQuarrie. "As it turns out, it's an animal that has to function in the snow! So I took back the beast and winterized it." Joe Johnston made further tauntaun sketches, coming up with an alternative, bird-like look. Pre-production proved

01 An early Ralph McQuarrie painting from February 1978, showing an early version of a tauntaun as concieved by George Lucas.

02

02 Ford, Fisher, and Hamill on location with a tauntaun! During early stages of production, a man in a suit was considered as a means to make the tauntaun come to life, before the idea was dropped in favor of a mechanical version of the creature.

03 Luke rides a tauntaun in this concept art by McQuarrie, 1979.

03

04

RM0161

05

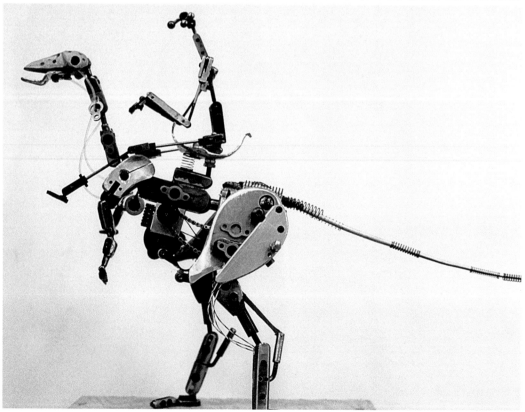

04 Another early
tauntaun concept by
McQuarrie (January
1978); early sketches
were partially influenced
by "Tyrannosaurus
and Triceratops" by
Charles Knight.

05 To make the
tauntaun move,
Doug Beswick and
Tom St. Amand worked
on a complex internal
mechanism with ball-
and-socket joints and
hinged skeletons.

06 Tauntaun sculpts
realized by stop-motion
animator Phil Tippett
during pre-production
in late 1978: the one
featuring the rider is
the design that would
eventually be approved.

06

equally challenging. At first, the tauntaun was to be portrayed by an actor in a suit, but the idea was soon discarded. The tauntaun sketches were eventually passed on to stop-motion animator Phil Tippett, who was working on the movie's stop-motion scenes. Tippett took over from where Johnston and McQuarrie had left off and came up with what would become the tauntaun's final design. As for how to make it come to life, "it was Lucas' decision to have something

more original looking than a guy fitted into a suit," said Tippett. "The final consideration was to get something that looked like a thing unto itself, rather than an object that looked dead or artificial." The coveted result was eventually achieved through a combination of filming techniques. To reach as much realism as possible to the stop-motion sequences, Tippett added a blurring effect to the frames: "What makes a running horse look real is the fact that the motion-picture

film is inadequately capturing the information of how he moves and is causing these blurs." For the Norway shots, the crew availed themselves of two different tauntauns: a full-body puppet and a 'half' one with just a head, neck and back operated by technicians during close-ups. To mimic the animal's steaming breath, gas was channeled to the tauntaun's mouth through two tubes. The final touch was made by recording a sea otter called Mota for the tauntaun's voice.

THE WAMPA – With an average height of 9 feet, a layer of woolly white fur—perfect for snow camouflage—large fangs and pointed claws, it is no mystery why wampas are the most dreaded creatures on Hoth. These huge, ruthless predators are well known to tauntauns, their main prey, and also to Luke Skywalker, who is attacked by a wampa while on patrol duties.

The ice creature was originally supposed to be called "penocha," but its name was changed to "wampa" in the second draft. Similarly to tauntauns, the making of the wampa entailed several turnarounds and subsequent difficulties. At first, the wampa was impersonated by actor Des Webb, who had to wear an enormous costume for the Hoth scenes shot in Norway. The suit, made of real sheepskin and fur, was extremely uncomfortable: Webb had to walk on stilts and would often fall after just a few steps, and the heat inside the costume was so unbearable that the crew had to regularly feed air to Webb through a tube

The full-scale costume was soon discarded in favor of a more functional puppet—made of just a head and torso—which was used to shoot the scene where the wampa screams right before attacking Luke. Additionally, a puppet hand, built by Tippett, was used in the close-up where Luke is struck by the wampa's paw.

Several sequences involving wampas did not make the final cut. Amongst these, a scene in which the wampa is seen inside Echo Base in three different moments: At first, its claws appear through an ice wall while Han Solo and Leia Organa are quarreling not too far away; then different wampas rampage in a corridor and are shot down by rebel troopers; finally, a wampa captures a snowtrooper who opens a door of the room where the creature is kept, after C-3PO removed the warning sign on it. According to the Progress Report, these shots, which required "the man inside the monster suit" to wear the costume for three hours straight, weren't good enough to make the final version of the movie. They would only be released on Blu-ray, in 2011.

07 Hamill as Skywalker inside the wampa's lair. After the scene had been planned by Kershner, the first unit team filmed for one day in the cave.

08 Tippett performs a dental examination on the wampa.

09 Bill Neil and Tippett film the wampa against a cloudy sky in the first months of 1980 for the scene in which the wampa roars at Luke on Hoth.

07

9

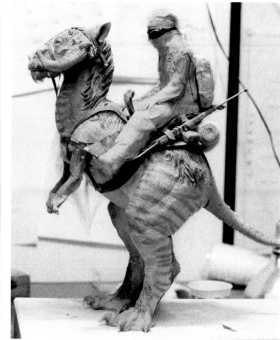

10

1

10 The cast of the tauntaun model created by Tippett. According to him the only way to make the tauntaun look like a living creature was with a small model, using stop-motion and motion-control techniques combined.

11 Tauntaun and rider. The ILM crew used a fellow crew member dressed as a tauntaun, running through the hangar for reference.

12 To keep Luke warm while they wait for help, Han stuffs him inside the innards of a dead tauntaun. This was, according to Kershner, an old Native American trick.

13 Han and his tauntaun in the midst of a snow storm. As he wasn't formally enlisted in the Rebel Alliance, Solo didn't wear the rebels' uniform.

1

15

14 A stop-motion puppet of Luke Skywalker atop his tauntaun in a snowstorm.

15 Tippett with a tiny model of the tauntaun, which was cast in a flexible material so that it'd be easy to work with.

16 Dennis Muren, Phil Tippett and matte artist Mike Pangrazio pose between two of Pangrazio's paintings.

16

17 A close-up of Luke Skywalker on his tauntaun moments before the wampa attacks him. According to art director Alan Tomkins , "The biggest problem with the tauntaun was the actual weight of the skin and the size of the head."

18

19

18 Han and Leia run towards the full-sized *Falcon* on the *Star Wars* Stage, which was used for the rebel hangar set and the Dagobah set.

19 "Don't lose your temper!" Upon entering the hangar, Solo is prompted by a rather irritated Chewbacca to help him operate a fusioncutter atop the *Millennium Falcon*.

20 The original prop of the *Falcon* built for the first film was no longer usable, so a new one—a full-size model this time—was manufactured in Pembrokshire, Wales. It was approximately 80 feet long.

21 The cockpit set proved particularly stressful for actors. As explained by Kurtz, "It was very close quarters to start with and a lot had to go on in there. And some of the action as written was very difficult to actually perform in the confines of the cockpit."

21

22

23

23 The smallest *Millennium Falcon* model ever created was specifically built for *The Empire Strikes Back*. Tiny enough to fit in the palm of a hand, the model was used for a scene where the *Falcon* docks against the outside of a Star Destroyer.

24 Chief model maker Michael Fulmer working on a 24-inch model of the *Falcon*.

25 ILM model makers Ease Owyeung and Michael Fulmer add greebles (fine details) to a 32-inch version of a *Millennium Falcon* model.

22 The *Millennium Falcon* in the docking bay of the rebel base on Hoth. Concept art by McQuarrie.

24

25

26 Harrison Ford on the set of the Hoth rebel base, near the *Millennium Falcon* landing gear.

27 Princess Leia and medical droid 2-1B check in on Luke in the Echo Base medical lab.

28 Leia listens to Han Solo's report in the Echo Base command center.

29 A production shot of Echo Base's main hangar.

30 Chewbacca despairs when Leia is forced to seal off the rebel base, leaving Han and Luke outside.

31 Chewbacca repairing the *Millennium Falcon*'s landing gear.

26

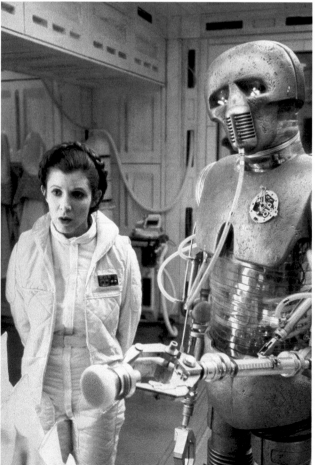

27

2

3

32 Carrie Fisher as Princess Leia in her snow outfit. The actress traveled to the Hoth location in Norway even though the scenes at Finse didn't require her. As explained by Kurtz, "She just could not bear to miss the location atmosphere."

33 Inside the ship's hold, Chewbacca strenuously tries to fix the hyperdrive mechanism.

34 The scenes set inside the cockpit of the *Millennium Falcon* were first shot looking back toward the cockpit; and then a month later, looking toward the bluescreen outside (shown here with a starfield).

4

35

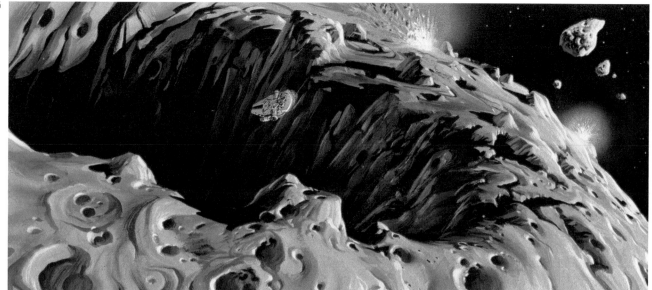

36

35 Trying to escape the Empire, the *Millennium Falcon* flies through an asteroid field and hides inside what seems to be a crater. Concept art by McQuarrie.

36 "Giant worm" (the space slug) by McQuarrie, July 20–21, 1978; the *Falcon*'s breakout scene shares some similarities with Pinocchio's escape from the whale's belly in the 1940's Disney adaptation.

37 Shooting the asteroid scene. When the cavern begins to shake, Han, Leia, and the others realize they are actually inside a giant space slug.

⊥ΞVＩ ⌐KﾘﾉＶＩフ

YODA

For more than 800 years, legendary Jedi Master Yoda trained countless generations of Jedi, including Obi-Wan Kenobi, and witnessed some of the most significant moments in the galaxy's history. At the end of the Clone Wars and with the formation of the Galactic Empire, Yoda went into hiding on Dagobah, a remote planet in the Outer Rim territories. His appearance and short stature (he is only 26 inches tall) could mislead those who judge individuals by their size and underestimate the power of the Force.

THE ORIGINS – During a story conference, which lasted from November 28 through December 2, 1977, George Lucas revealed his plan to feature "a new teacher" in *The Empire Strikes Back*. "Instead of a withered old man, we can use a withered old space creature. The way to think of it is as this crazy little nitwit who scurries around like a rat, that in the end teaches Luke a lot of stuff about the Force." The creature Lucas had in mind was "tiny, slightly froglike with slick skin, wide mouth, no nose and bulbous eyes that move around." In the treatment that followed the conference, the creature was named "Minch Yoda." Originally, Minch Yoda was supposed to star alongside Alec Guinness, who'd be returning as Obi-Wan Kenobi; unfortunately, due to health problems, the actor was forced to withdraw, thus making the role of Yoda much more prominent. "One of the challenges was I had to replace Obi-Wan Kenobi," Lucas would comment. "I wanted something like Guinness; I wanted to transfer his performance into Yoda, so I worked on Yoda with Joe Johnston at first. I wanted someone very old and very unassuming." In Johnston's early sketches, which date back to February 1978, Yoda resembled a tiny, Santa

01 Luke meets Yoda for the first time. In his early development, Yoda was conceived as an eight- or nine-foot-tall bearded Zen master; as explained by Kershner, the idea was discarded as "too much of a cliché."

Claus-like creature. The near-final concept was eventually achieved by combining the design of a leprechaun, a troll and a gnome, thanks to which Yoda gained what would become some of his most iconic traits: large ears and head; green skin and three-toed hands and feet. A further peculiarity was added in the second draft, when Lucas developed a specific speech style for Yoda: "I felt his dialogue and cadence should be unique... I had to come up with something that's not a foreign language, not an accent, but somewhere in between those two things. That's how I started Yoda's backward style." In the third-draft script, writer Lawrence Kasdan added wit to Yoda's lines, while in the fourth draft Yoda's prop, a pipe, was replaced with a "Gimer Stick." Whilst the visual characterization was being finalized, the question remained regarding how to physically bring Yoda to life...

03 On Dagobah, Yoda engages in a fight with R2-D2 over a tiny power lamp. This was also Mark Hamill and Frank Oz's first scene together.

04 Yoda challenges Luke to overcome his physical limits and feel the Force surrounding him.

05 Master Yoda uses the Force to lift Luke's X-wing out of a swamp on Dagobah.

06 Originally, special creature designer Stuart Freeborn wanted Yoda to have a little mustache, but it didn't seem quite right; he eventually added an almost unnoticeable shape of a mustache to his bottom lip.

07 An astonished Skywalker gazes at the X-wing starfighter being raised from the waters of Dagobah.

03

04

05

06

07

08

MAKING YODA – To bring Yoda to the screen, Lucas reached out to Jim Henson, who was gaining popularity as the creator of *The Muppets*. Lucas wanted Henson to help them create a realistic puppet of Yoda, but due to other work commitments Henson couldn't take him up on the offer, so he recommended another skilled puppeteer: his co-worker Frank Oz. As explained by Lucas, Oz was pivotal in helping them bring Yoda to life as "he helped technically evolve the puppet in a way he would really be able to act with it." The physical puppet was built by makeup and special creature designer Stuart Freeborn, who had developed several masks—including Chewbacca's—for *A New Hope*. Quite curiously, Freeborn started off by modifying a clay sculpture of his own head; to convey the character's wisdom and intelligence, he added ridges to the statue and provided the "little fellow" with "Einstein's eyes." Once the sculpting design was approved, he then fabricated the puppet with the help of Wendy Midener.

Yoda arrived on set on Monday, August 6, 1979, putting the whole crew under extreme pressure ("If that puppet didn't work, the whole film was going to fail," Lucas would later comment). Indeed, the work proved to be challenging as well as exhausting: the puppet's features were so advanced that, in some instances, four people had to operate it at the same time, and a single line would take hours of rehearsal and preparation. On top of that, Mark Hamill couldn't hear Yoda's voice as his earpiece never worked, so he had to act in front of a completely silent puppet; to get the timing right, he would rehearse each scene with a speaker beforehand. With regards to Yoda's voice-over, Oz was eventually chosen to dub the Jedi Master. At first

09

08 Luke training with his lightsaber (before special effects were added) on Dagobah. The scene was eventually cut from the film. Skywalker's training entailed climbing, jumping, flipping and racing in and out of the swamp planet's misty forests.

09 Luke stands on one hand while balancing his master on one foot. Shots featuring Yoda demanded a lot of concentration from actors and crew alike.

Lucas was quite reluctant to the idea as he didn't want Yoda to sound like Miss Piggy, Oz's famous Muppet character. However, he soon realized no one would be able to perform Yoda as well as Oz. "I wanted to use a different actor. But I've discovered over the years that, in terms of puppetry, the person who is actually acting the role is really into it."

If bringing Yoda to life and working with him had been emotionally hard, parting ways was even harder. As recounted

by Kershner, "Not only is Luke saying goodbye to Yoda, but the audience is saying goodbye to him... you know you're not going to be seeing him again, and it's kind of sad because you like him." Lucas would further add, "Kersh did a great job with Yoda. He never thought of him as a puppet." Ultimately, the key secret to Yoda's success as a character is that neither did the audience: everyone believed he was real and that he was teaching Luke the ways of the Force. ☠

DAGOBAH

With a surface almost entirely covered in foggy swamps and muddy bogs, the small and almost forgotten planet of Dagobah never offered the best conditions for a permanent settlement. To the untrained eye, its dreary and humid landscape may seem completely devoid of life, while in fact so many creatures, such as bogwings, butcherbugs, and dragonsnakes, hide and thrive beyond its floating mists. Home to Master Yoda in his last years of exile, Dagobah is incredibly strong in the Force; this makes it an excellent location for whoever is seeking Jedi training.

THE ORIGIN – The planet Dagobah, often referred to as "bog planet," was amongst the earliest ideas George Lucas had for the film. It came around in *The Empire Strikes Back* story conference as the potential "place where Luke learns" and, according to Lucas, it was supposed to be "very swampy, very eerie and misty, like *Hound of the Baskervilles.*" Originally, a few locations in Central Africa had been considered for shooting the Dagobah scenes, but the idea was discarded in favor of an on-site sound stage whose construction started in early 1978. The stage was going to be 250 feet long, 122 feet wide, and 45 feet high, in the hope that it would accommodate both the rebel hangar and the bog planet sets.

Yet, cohabitation between two separate environments proved quite difficult. As explained by Kershner, scenes were shot "on those parts of the *Star Wars* Stage which had been finished, using more and more space as it became available. When the whole stage was finally completed, the process reversed somewhat… Some days I would come onto the set and find that an ice corridor had become a swamp overnight."

01 "It's really a strange place to find a Jedi Master." Luke Skywalker lands on the swamp planet of Dagobah, looking for Yoda.

02 Mark Hamill as Luke Skywalker trains with Master Yoda. On set, gnarltrees were made with wire mesh and plaster.

03 Luke and Yoda walk through the misty forests on Dagobah in a production illustration by Ralph McQuarrie, 1979.

03

04 Yoda's hut concept art by Ralph McQuarrie. The early design for the gnarltrees was based on the giant banyan trees.

05 The interior of Yoda's hut as originally envisioned by McQuarrie.

06 According to production designer Norman Reynolds, "Yoda's house is perhaps a hangover from Tunisia, where there are some buildings that are built in this sort of way."

07 Luke eats a bowl of Yoda's rootleaf stew inside the Jedi Master's home. Mark Hamill is sitting on a platform so that Frank Oz can operate the Yoda puppet from underneath.

04

06

05

07

08

PROBLEMS ON SET – In early July 1979, upon completion of the *Millennium Falcon* sequences, the construction and art departments resumed building the bog planet set on the *Star Wars* Stage. Due to budgetary reasons, they had to construct Dagobah in half the time originally scheduled—that is seven weeks instead of fourteen—and the crew had to work at night and over weekends. To further optimize the time left, Lucas rewrote the storyboards and got down to a number of shots which could actually be completed within that specific time frame; as a result, several scenes had to be shortened and reworked. The bog set was particularly challenging in terms of both design and physical development, and was still in the making while filming started: "We had to start in the back corner with some of the smaller scenes and work our way out to the tank part where the lake was," explained Gary Kurtz, vice president of

production on *Star Wars*.

The bog planet was specifically designed to resemble a real-life location: "The ground was real earth, real mud, real water… It was extremely muddy and we used a lot of smoke for fog and mist," recounted associate producer Robert Watts. "We had a real river running, with real animals and everything," added Kurtz. "We had a lot of snakes—and some of them got away and started inhabiting the set. Birds flew through the doors of the sound stage and, because of the grass and dirt that was brought in, we had bugs and spiders and things. It became a real place."

Gulls, terns, sea lions and dolphins, amongst the others, were recorded for the bog's wildlife. Similarly to humans, some animals were quite drained by the hard work on the bog set. On one occasion, whilst filming the 'Yoda's revelation' scene, a snake nipped Hamill, perhaps as a protest to the numerous takes they had to go through. Indeed, the set itself was so tricky and

technically challenging that filming a few seconds would sometimes take a whole day or more—an example is the scene where the Jedi Master uses the Force to lift Luke's X-wing out of the swamp.

Despite everyone doing their best, Kershner wasn't fully satisfied with his own work: "The bog planet is an extraordinarily difficult set," he admitted. "The terrible thing is, here is this expensive, really quite almost insanely expensive picture, and yet I have to compromise all the way down the line… I'm sure that the audience won't know the difference, but in my eyes, it's quite different."

Physically exhausted, the crew officially finished filming *Empire* on the afternoon of September 24, 1979, with an insert of Luke on Hoth and a scene in the swamps of the bog planet. But matte paintings, visual effects, sound effects, and stop-motion flying creatures still had to be added to make Dagobah come to life. ☙

08 R2-D2 peeps through a window of Yoda's hut. Conceived by Kershner, this is one of Lucas' favorite moments in the film.

09 To shoot Darth Vader's "unmasking" in Dagobah's cave sequence, a mold of Mark Hamill's head was originally considered—it was, however, soon discarded in favor of Hamill's real head. The shot was in fact achieved with Hamill's face popping out of a hole in the stage floor as he stood below it.

10 After several weeks of filming, the bog swamp had become quite filthy. "I have to say, you wouldn't want to fall in that pool," said production designer Norman Reynolds. Of course, at least one crew member fell in.

9

10

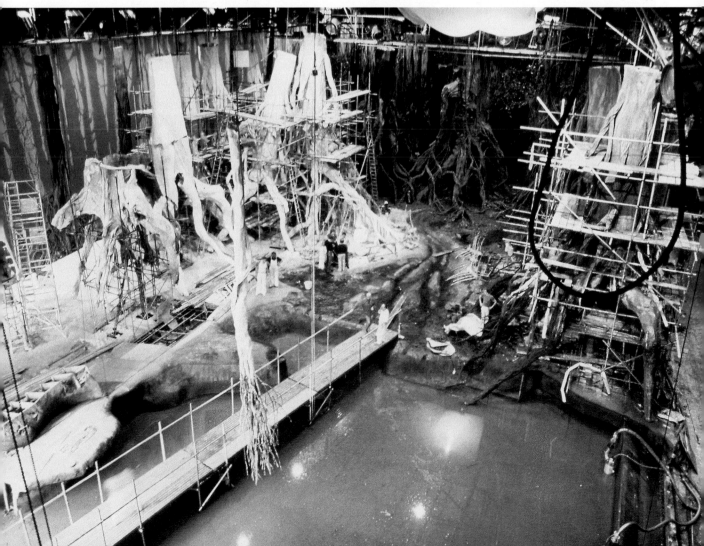

11 "I don't... I don't believe it," says Luke Skywalker staring in astonishment as his X-wing settles onto the shore. "That is why you fail," replies Master Yoda. Shot on September, 1979, this scene required more than six hours to film.

ꓳꓱꓦ�1 ꓬ1ꓩꓩꓘ1ꓥ

THE EMPEROR

After having only been mentioned in *A New Hope*, The Emperor made his chilling screen debut in *The Empire Strikes Back*. The hooded figure with the eerily hideous face appeared for just a minute, and only in the form of a hologram. But his cameo appearance was used to great effect. Even the formidable Darth Vader bowed before him. It was proof that the enemy Luke, Leia, and Han were running from actually lived in fear of someone else… someone who had to be much more powerful! But as we all know, and as George Lucas himself admitted, the best way to create a supervillain is "to take the biggest villain you've got and make him afraid of the supervillain."

THE ORIGIN – It had been clear that the Emperor would be the saga's main villain ever since *Star Wars: A New Hope*. After all, if there's a Galactic Empire, there must also be an Emperor to reign over it. Darth Vader, however much he comes off as the number one adversary facing the protagonists, would soon become only a cog, albeit a crucial one, in the machine of oppression. From Leigh Brackett's first draft in 1977, which first introduces the Emperor based on Lucas' outline, to the fifth draft by Lawrence Kasdan in 1979, the Emperor would however remain shadowy and obscure in *The Empire Strikes Back*. Lucas knew that any appearances by the Emperor would have to be carefully measured in the wake of his existence in *A New Hope*. A transcription of the back story conference held on November 28 through December 2, 1977 revealed Lucas saying, "He's

not as dramatic as Vader, but is more sinister. Vader is just one of his lap dogs. Do we show the Emperor this time or wait until the next one where we finally confront him? How about if we don't see his face?" All the same, his brief appearance in *The Empire Strikes Back* would give audiences a chance to actually see this mysterious and wicked manipulator, one Lucas himself imagined as a cross between a gloomy Wizard of Oz and Richard Nixon. The Emperor, whose true identity would be one of the longest kept secrets of the entire *Star Wars* saga, would represent the ultimate enemy, whose defeat would coincide with the saga's conclusion. Lucas' earliest notes in a yellow legal pad highlighted the importance of such a defeat: "Emperor/Empire must be destroyed; restore the Republic." However, the confrontation between Luke and the character that we would later know as either Darth Sidious or Sheev Palpatine, was still on the distant horizon. For the time being, the

Emperor's importance need only be defined, which could be done merely by pointing out his position in the Imperial hierarchy. In a scene that was cut from *The Empire Strikes Back*, the discussion between Darth Vader and the Emperor's hologram is preceded by another scene. Between the second and the fourth draft, Palpatine is introduced by another character, Sate Pestage, who presents him as "Grand Vizier to His Eminence, The Emperor." In the second draft, where initially he was called Sate Molock, he warns Darth Vader that the Emperor is in a bad mood, before letting the Emperor speak. Sate's presence via hologram would remain until the fourth draft, after which the character was dropped and the scene deleted. Darth Vader directly addresses the Emperor, apparently without any go-betweens. That decision underscores the importance of their master-pupil relationship and renders the role of Darth Vader even more prominent within the Imperial hierarchy.

01 Darth Vader faces the terrifying presence of the Emperor's hologram.

02 The Emperor in a still which first appeared in the 2004 DVD release of the movie. For this edition, the original actress was substituted with Ian McDarmind. The British actor debuted as the Emperor in *Return of the Jedi* (1983), and then reprised the role of Palpatine in the prequel trilogy (1999-2005) and *The Rise of Skywalker* (2019).

03

In the script, the Emperor is presented as the counterpart to hero Luke Skywalker's mentor, Obi-Wan Kenobi, and is depicted as someone even more frightful than Darth Vader: "The Emperor's dark robes and monk's hood are reminiscent of the cloak worn by Ben Kenobi. His voice is even deeper and more frightening than Vader's."

THE SET – The appearance of the Emperor meant another problem to solve: What would he look like under his hood? Lucas opted for the face of a woman, the character actress Marjorie Eaton (1901-1986), with the gaunt visage, prominent nose and high cheekbones. She wore a mask sculpted by Phil Tippett. In test

runs, the mask was initially applied by makeup artist Rick Baker to his wife Elaine's face. The eyes of a chimpanzee were later superimposed in the shadow of the hood, after having experimented with a cat's eyes and the eyes of assistant accountant Laura Crockett. The chimp's eyes and the Emperor's face were combined using a split-beam technique and a mirror. The voice would be that of actor Clive Revill. Unfortunately, Marjoire Eaton received no screen credit for her role. The hologram was added during post-production in the huge room where Darth Vader had made his bow before nothing during filming. As effects specialist Ken Ralston explains,

"To make the hologram of the Emperor, we shot an actor in makeup with the eyes blacked out. We wound up shooting the eyes of a chimpanzee, then matchmoving the eyes of the actor and rephotographing it from a TV screen. Actually, that was true of all the hologram shots." The Emperor character would go on to become a central focus of the entire saga, and that began with those few seconds in *The Empire Strikes Back*. In *Return of the Jedi* the Emperor was portrayed by the British actor Ian McDiarmid for the first time. McDiarmid returned in the role of Palpatine in *The Phantom Menace*, *Attack of the Clones*, *Revenge of the Sith*, and *The Rise of Skywalker*. As for the Emperor's brief appearance in

03 The Emperor's fleet in pursuit of the rebels in a composite image. The huge Star Destroyer model posed with some other models, most notably the one for the *Millennium Falcon*, in front of a blue screen.

04 Special effects supervisor Brian Johnson posing with the massive 10-foot Star Destroyer model. A new version of these massive ships would later appear in the saga, including in *Return of the Jedi*, along with the resurrected Emperor.

05 Chief model maker Lorne Peterson and art director Joe Johnston looking at the work in progress of the Star Destroyer's control tower.

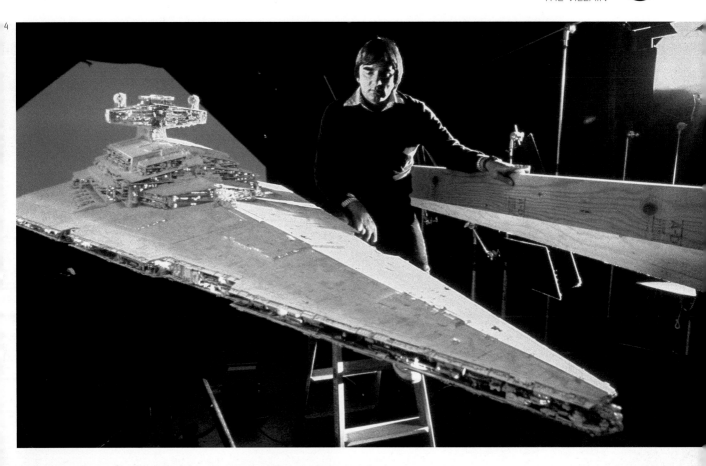

06

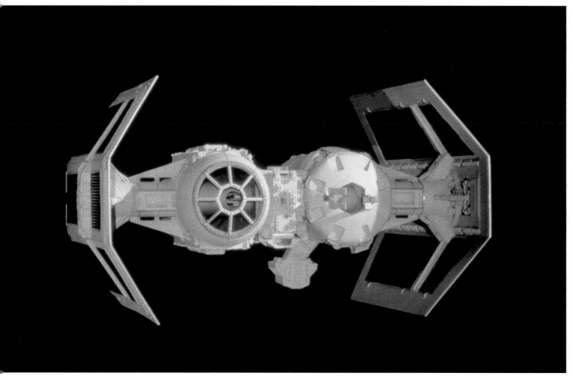

06 Effects cameraman Ken Ralston moving a battle-damaged Tie Fighter. Dennis Muren, effects director of photography, said about him, "His maneuvering of the TIE fighter and the *Falcon* show his great understanding of the need for timing, motion, and life within the shot."

07 The TIE bomber, which debuted in *The Empire Strikes Back*, is one of the many variations of TIE starfighters in the Imperial Navy. While most are known for their speed and agility, this one is known for its powerful ordnance.

08 For *The Empire Strikes Back*, the model department prepared several TIE fighters and those ships are featured extensively in the movie.

07

The Empire Strikes Back, Eaton's face was digitally replaced by that of McDiarmid for the 2004 DVD release. That version included new dialogue featuring the voices of Ian McDiarmid, replacing that of Clive Revill, and James Earl Jones, who voiced Darth Vader. Re-shoots were done during filming for *Revenge of the Sith*. Over the years, *Star Wars* fans would come to learn and fear the name Palpatine, they would follow his devious exploits as both Senator and Supreme Chancellor Palpatine, and would wind up mesmerized by his return and the many revelations he would bring with him in *The Rise of Skywalker*. ☮

08

09

09 Jeremy Bulloch
(on the right), the
man under the helmet
of Boba Fett, also
portrayed Lieutenant
Scheckil.

10 Kenneth Colley
plays Admiral Piett.
He replaces Kendal
Ozzel when he's
punished by Vader.

11 Michael Sheard
plays Admiral Kendal
Ozzel, who was the
commanding officer
of the *Executor*.

12 "Apology accepted,
Captain Needa." Darth
Vader (David Prowse)
stands over the body of
the inept Lorth Needa
(Michael Culver). Vader
strangled Needa after
he let the *Millennium
Falcon* escape.

10

11

13/14

13/14 Concepts by
Ralph McQuarrie for
the bridge of the Super
Star Destroyer *Executor*,
Darth Vader's command
ship.

15 In this unfinished
shot, the final result
of the bridge of the
Executor is darker
than in the concept
by McQuarrie.

16 A model maker
caught by the camera
while adding the final
touches to the Super
Star Destroyer,
the *Executor*.

15

‹Star Wars Aurebesh text›

BOBA FETT

Gathering aboard the Super Star Destroyer, the *Executor*,
at the behest of Darth Vader are some of the galaxy's most
feared bounty hunters. Offering a generous reward for whoever
finds the *Millennium Falcon* and its crew, Vader singles out one of
the motley bunch, and issues the directive, "I want them alive.
No disintegrations..." The helmeted warrior is Boba Fett,
who coolly replies: "As you wish."

HE ORIGIN – Despite having very few lines of dialogue, and without ever having his name mentioned during the movie, aside from a deleted scene where Leia is tending Luke's wounds and she says Han has been captured by "a bounty hunter named Boba Fett," the character has remained one of the most popular characters among fans of *Star Wars* since first appearing in *The Empire Strikes Back*. And since that debut, few characters have generated the kind of fan dedication and inspired the amount of stories that Boba Fett has. For decades fans speculated as to his origins, at least until *Attack of the Clones* (2002). And to think that initially he had been no more than a work-in-progress version of Darth Vader. "There were quite a few films made about bounty hunters in the Old West," said George Lucas, "that's where that came from. When I was writing the early scripts for *Star Wars*, I wanted to develop an essentially evil character that was frightening. Darth Vader started as a kind of intergalactic bounty hunter in a space suit and evolved into a more grotesque

01 The lineup of bounty hunters aboard Darth Vader's command ship included a humanoid, Dengar; an assassin droid, IG-88; Boba Fett; a Trandoshan, Bossk; a protocol-droid-turned-mercenary 4-LOM; and a Gand, Zuckuss. In the script, reptile-looking Bossk was originally described as "a slimy, tentacled monster with two huge, bloodshot eyes in a soft baggy face".

02 A prototype of Boba Fett's outfit. In addition to armor and other necessary gear, it is also adorned with what looks to be braids of hair, which have been described in the past as belonging to Wookiees he has defeated.

knight as I got more into knights and the codes of everything. He became more of a Dark Lord than a mercenary bounty hunter. The Boba Fett character is really an early version of Darth Vader. He is also very much like the man-with-no-name from the Sergio Leone Westerns." Indeed, Boba Fett would retain the quiet attitude and the cloak reminiscent of the legendary character played by Clint Eastwood. Other elements of the character's iconic look date back to concepts that had been previously scrapped. Several touches were added to his helmet, taken from Ralph McQuarrie's 1975 sketches. To a certain degree, that helmet recalled a samurai mask, and some parts, like the chin and the mouth, were later used for Darth Vader's mask. Together, his costume and helmet also take inspiration from an elite caste of stormtroopers. These super-stormtroopers were better equipped and more thoroughly prepared for combat than

03

03 Boba Fett's helmet was an evolution of an unused concept. Originally, he was going to be part of a group of supertroopers, or super-stormtroopers, who would be dressed in all-white armor.

04 Visual effects art director Joe Johnston defining the details on Boba Fett's helmet.

04

05

06

regular soldiers. Their armor was all-white, their helmets were slightly different. Another version of Boba Fett may be seen in Prince Valorum, Black Knight of the Sith, who appeared in Lucas' first draft for *Star Wars* as one of Darth Vader's henchmen, who was sent out to capture rebels. In March 1978, all these ideas were blended together by George Lucas, Ralph McQuarrie, and Joe Johnston, to create the bounty hunter we know. Boba Fett was a "real villain", who would sell his services to the highest bidder, like Bossk, IG-88 and the other bad guys who appeared alongside Darth Vader.

BEHIND THE MASK – Boba Fett's famed armor was painted by Johnston, based on a precise idea: "It was a symmetrical design, but I painted it in such a way that it looked like he had scavenged parts and

done some personalizing of his costume; he had little trophies hanging from his belt, little braids of hair, almost like a collection of scalps." Once the armor was ready, it was tried out by Duwayne Dunham, assistant film editor for *The Empire Strikes Back* and *Return of the Jedi*. It also included a flamethrower built by Industrial Light & Magic, which, on its first test run, leaked and wound up scorching Dunham. The CO_2 cannister inside the backpack did work though. At any rate, the idea of the flamethrower would resurface later on. Thirty-five-year-old Jeremy Bulloch, associate producer Robert Watts' half-brother, was called in to play Boba Fett.

"I rang him up and said, 'If the suit fits, the part's yours,'" explained Watts. Bulloch got the part. For each round of shooting it took him 20 minutes

05 The infamous Boba Fett flamethrower, which burnt assistant film editor Duwayne Dunham while trying the costume.

06 Boba Fett's cape was based on Clint Eastwood's western hero, the Man With No Name.

to put on his costume. In the beginning he was bewildered by all the suit's gadgets and working parts: "There was an odd sort of Wookiee scalp hanging from my shoulder, which I originally put under my helmet because I thought it was some kind of hairpiece!" But Bulloch would not be the only one to wear Boba Fett's costume, as two more actors would also be playing the role. John Morton donned the armor in several scenes on Bespin, and in a few scenes of *Return of the Jedi* stuntman Dickey Beer filled in. Ten years later, Mark Austin

07

07 Boba Fett's ship, *Slave I*, was originally based on a radar dish, according to assistant art director Nilo Rodis-Jamero, "For some reason, when I drew it, George Lucas thought it was elliptical, so that's what it became."

08 Chief model maker Lorne Peterson and model maker Ease Owyeung working on a model of *Slave I*, built to be used with the blue screen.

09 Harrison Ellenshaw working on a matte painting of Boba Fett's ship, *Slave I*. It was included in the Cloud City scenes.

and Don Bies shared the role of Boba Fett in additional footage for the Special Edition re-releases. In post-production for *The Empire Strikes Back*, Bulloch's lines were dubbed by deep-voiced Jason Wingreen. And when the link between Boba and his "father" Jango Fett, whom he had been cloned from, was revealed, Temeura Morrison dubbed over Wingreen's voice work to underscore the connection.

All Boba Fett needed to make him even more independent was a ship all of his own. Assistant art director Nilo Rodis-Jamero, who had already designed the

Super Star Destroyer *Executor*, conceived what would become known as *Slave I*, Boba Fett's attack craft, different from anything seen up till then. Not much more was shown in *The Empire Strikes Back* and fans would have to wait decades to learn more about the bounty hunter, such as: the fact that he is a clone, the origins of his Mandalorian armor, his connection with Han Solo, and the trauma he suffered after Jango was killed by Mace Windu.

THE APPEARANCES – Actually, *The Empire Strikes Back* did

not mark the character's first appearance. As many fans know, Boba Fett first appeared in animated form, in a sequence of the 1978 *Star Wars Holiday Special*. To be precise, not even that bizarre occasion, where he is armed with a lance and wearing a blue helmet, was a true first. On September 24, 1978 Boba Fett appeared in the flesh alongside Darth Vader at the annual Country Fair Parade in San Anselmo, California, in Marin County, 20 miles north of San Francisco. Since 1971 the first Lucasfilm headquarters had been located

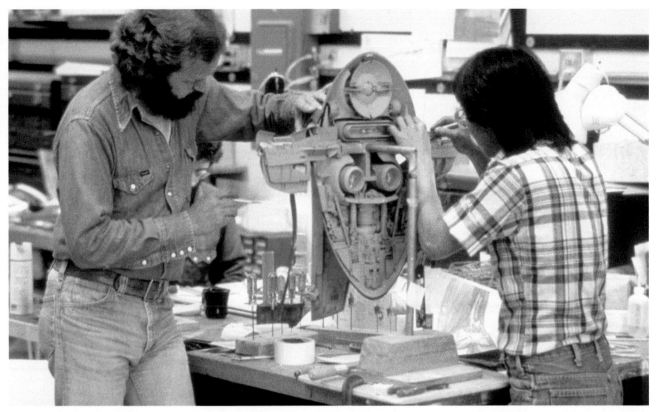

08

09

in the small city, at 52 Park Way. Lucasfilm wanted to pay tribute to the town it called home by including the most famous *Star Wars* characters in the parade. Duwayne Dunham, who'd been burned by the leaky flamethrower, wore Boba Fett's armor that day. At the time of the accident, the suit was just a prototype and missing a few details. Duwayne had been chosen at the last minute because it fit him. "What I remember about that day," he later recalled on *StarWars. com*, "is, it was incredibly hot. I'm not just talking about the suit, I'm saying that day in San Anselmo was really hot. It could have been 100 degrees. I think we were at the head of the parade. And Vader, he stands out. I don't know what people thought of me. Nobody knew about Boba Fett at that point!"

Almost at the same time, the team at Kenner who created *Star Wars* action figures had been pushing for new characters when they found out that the sequel to the original *Star Wars* wouldn't be coming out for another couple years. One of the characters they decided to develop during that time was Boba Fett. The first figure would be available as a mail-order item, available to kids months before the toy would hit store shelves. The prototype included a rocket that could be fired from the bounty hunter's backpack. But that extra was dropped for safety reasons. In the final version of the Boba Fett action figure, the rocket is incorporated and cannot be fired. As for the prototype, which was never marketed to the public, it is estimated that less than 30 remain in existence today. It is considered one of the rarest toys ever, and according to some estimates, this 3.75-inch piece of plastic is worth around $250,000. ☙

10 Lando Calrissian is finally getting a "bad feeling" about Darth Vader and Fett! In this scene, the walls of the corridor have been painted from white to red-brown, in order to show different rooms using the same set.

11 In Ralph McQuarrie's concept for the Cloud City prison, Boba Fett (right) is still wearing white armor.

12 Boba Fett escorting the defeated Han Solo. The Cloud City guards behind him are Quentin Pierre (left) and Alan Harris (right). Harris played several minor roles in the saga, including Bossk.

1

12

13

14

13 David Prowse
(Darth Vader),
Morris Bush (Dengar),
mechanical puppet
IG-88, Jeremy Bulloch
(Boba Fett) and Alan
Harris (Bossk) on
the bridge of Vader's
Star Destroyer.

14 Former boxer
Morris Bush, who
plays bounty hunter
Dengar, played
alongside Christopher
Lee in *Scars of Dracula*
(1970) and The
Creeping Flesh (1973).

15 A detailed shot
of IG-88. The assassin
droid puppet was
constructed by Bill
Hargreaves and
Steve Short.

⨯∃⼍ ⼂⼍⼊⼂∃⼁⼍⼐

LANDO CALRISSIAN

"How you doin', ya old pirate? So good to see ya!" When he welcomes Han Solo and the rebels in search of refuge, there are plenty of hugs, smiles and compliments, and Lando Calrissian appears to be an ally they can trust, a friend. Then comes his betrayal, which would impact this character's every move from then on. But there's more to the story behind Lando Calrissian, a key *Star Wars* character in a compromised position. Elegant and sophisticated, almost as to be out of place with respect to the other rebels, a guy who gambles with life the way he bets at sabacc, Lando has remained in fans' hearts. And his role in the saga after *The Empire Strikes Back* would become increasingly crucial, all the way to the height of his endeavors to advance the cause of the Rebel Alliance in the finale of *Return of the Jedi*.

THE ORIGIN – The first two new characters introduced in *The Empire Strike Back* could be pigeonholed into precise categories. Yoda is an altogether positive figure, a good mentor. Boba Fett is an anti-hero, more bad than good. Then there's the third new character, Lando Calrissian, who appears to be a villainous sort at first, but evolves and becomes one of the good guys. If Lando's character arc is complex, the conception and development of the character were no less so. At a story conference held from November 28 through December 2, 1977, George Lucas described him to Leigh Brackett as such: "He's a slick, riverboat gambler type of dude. Han Solo is a rather crude, rough and tumble kind of guy; this guy will be a very slicked down, elegant, James Bond–type. He's much more of a con man, which puts him more in the Mr. Spock style of thinking, being smart, cool, and taking tremendous chances." Unlike Han and Chewie, from the start Lando takes on the role of strategist and foregoes the role of combatant. "He's someone who uses his wits rather than his brawn. He could be a gambler friend of Han Solo's. They're both underworld characters." Even his initial ambiguity was a factor that Lucas had decided upon from the very beginning. "This guy will have asome kind of relationship with the Empire. He'll be pro-Empire, but he thinks he's smarter than the Empire. He doesn't really care about the Rebellion, but, in the end, he realizes that he must join the Rebellion and that the Empire is terrible."

Once characterization had been defined, it was time to imagine what Lando might look like. For the concept, Lucas went back to an idea that had only roughly been sketched out. There had already been an allusion to it in *A New Hope* —a reference to an imaginary "Clone War." Lando… could have been one of the clones. When the character was still nameless, Lucas proposed: "Maybe he could look human but not really be human. He's possibly a clone. We talked earlier about the Clone Wars. The princess doesn't trust him because of that; Leia might refer to him in a derogatory way. If we set him up as a clone, maybe in one of the other Episodes, we can have him run across a clan who are all exactly like him. We won't go into the whole mythology of where they came from or whether the clones were good or bad. We'll assume that they were slightly weird in their own way and were partly responsible for the war. We'll assume that on these planets of clones, there are many countries, say about 700 countries, and he's from one of the ruling clone clans."

01 There's history between Han Solo and Lando, which is only hinted upon in *Empire*. It will be explored only many years later in *Solo: A Star Wars Story* (2018). In the prequel, Alden Ehrenreich plays Han and Donald Glover plays Lando.

02 Lando immediately shows his charm upon meeting Princess Leia for the first time, much to the dismay of Han.

02

03

03 According to Billy Dee Williams, Lando Calrissian betrayed Han Solo because "He was trying to prevent the demise of Han Solo and his friends, because he had no choice".

04 The infamous dinner scene. Opposite the table, Darth Vader is challenging his enemies. Han and Leia hold hands, while Lando starts to regret his choices...

That idea was eventually axed, but it did make it as far as Leigh Brackett's first draft of the script. There too, Han and Leia go to a city in the clouds in search of Lando. Back then he was known as Lando Kadar, and was accompanied by Bahiri, chief of the White Bird clan of the Cloud People. In that version, Lando soon confessed to Han and Leia the secret of his origins. In Brackett's script he tells them, "I'm a clone. Of the Ashardi family. My great-grandfather wanted many sons and he produced them from the cells of his own body. His sister, a remarkable woman, produced many daughters by the same means. Thus, we keep the blood pure. But since the wars, there are not many of us left and we try not to attract attention."

THE ACTOR – One feature that remained unchanged was Lando's style and grace, which are in stark contrast with the gloomy, grimy back-drops seen up till now. At first, Lucas described him "as a Rudolph Valentino character, 1930s hair, slicked back. Wears white sport coats, white carnations, always wheeling and dealing like a gambler. Sly. Make him almost too perfect looking." Some of his perfection was due to the fact that he is a clone: "We assume that in the cloning process, they manipulated genes and improved on the original."

Casting Lando, who in the meantime had evolved from gambler to entrepreneur, was not easy. The part was first offered to Yaphet Kotto,

who had played Dennis Parker in *Alien* (Ridley Scott, 1979). He turned it down, amid fears that the character would wind up killed, and instead opted for a part in the prison drama *Brubaker* (Stuart Rosenberg, 1980) alongside Robert Redford. Production turned its sights on another actor, Billy Dee Williams. With lengthy experience on Broadway and appearances in hit movies like *Brian's Song*, *Lady Sings the Blues* (1971), in which he played Louis McKay, Billie Holiday's husband) and *Mahogany* (1975) behind him, Williams had already been in touch with production. And when he won the role of Lando Calrissian, Billy Dee Williams and his seductive gaze became known to sci-fi fans. Cast

6

and crew looked forward to shooting his debut scene, which from a scenographic perspective was a complex one. What wound up in the film, however, is a little different to the script. When Lando eyes the princess with a little too much interest, Han was supposed to say, "She's traveling with me, Lando. And I don't intend to gamble her away, so you might as well forget she exists," as a way of underscoring his jealousy. Instead, Ford improvized and cut it short, and came back with, "You old smoothie"— words that have since stuck to the Lando Calrissian character like glue. Thus begins the character arc of the Cloud City gambler, one that would lead him to redemption. As Lucas said: "You have Lando who is

selling out his friends to save his city, and then you have Han and Leia caught in the middle of the whole mess." Adding, "Lando's decision to save his people and himself is a little like Han's development in *Star Wars* but also like Luke's, where fate steps in: He can't avoid the situation." The character reappeared on several other occasions becoming one of the saga's main heroes. Billy Dee Williams came back to play him in *Return of the Jedi*, where Lando destroys the second Death Star, and in *The Rise of Skywalker*. The actor also voiced Lando Carlissian in *Star Wars: Rebels* (2014 to 2018) animated series and in the videogames *Star Wars* Battlefront (2004) and Battlefront II (2017). Actor and musician Donald Glover played young Lando in the prequel *Solo: A Star Wars Story* (2018). It's been skyward all the way, ever since Williams burst onto the scene as Lando 40 years ago. ☘

05 Lando stares at the tragic process that freezes Han in carbonite. Behind them there are some Ugnaughts. One of the "Hogmen" appearing in the movie is played by Eileen Baker, the wife of Kenny Baker (R2-D2).

06 Han being frozen in carbonite finally prompted Lando to definitively choose a side in the Galactic Civil War. Things will never be the same for the smooth scoundrel, nor for Cloud City.

07 Chewie, Leia and Lando in the cockpit of the *Millennium Falcon*, surrounded by blue screen in Stage 8. The heroes are running from the Empire!

7

ᐯᕮᒋ ᑕᒍᔑᗅᐯᕲᒍᔑ

CLOUD CITY

Among the new settings seen in *The Empire Strikes Back*, audiences have always been awestruck by Cloud City. Hovering in the atmosphere above the planet Bespin, this sleek, high-tech town is the beating heart of the impressive gas giant. Besides serving as a mining colony, which made its fortune harvesting coveted tibanna gas from the planet's core, Cloud City was for many years considered a safe haven for anyone fleeing the clutches of the Empire. This is where Han, Leia, and Chewie seek refuge and Lando's help, before they realize that Darth Vader arrived there before them. Amid the corridors and conduits of Cloud City, the revelation that is perhaps most central to the entire saga is disclosed, transforming this almost dreamlike backdrop into one of the most significant locations in the saga. But originally the city ruled by Lando Calrissian was meant to be something else entirely...

THE CITY – In the early drafts of the script for *The Empire Strikes Back*, airborne Cloud City was an imperial prison. Back then it floated above a planet called Hoth—the name that would eventually be used for the ice planet seen in the opening sequence—and not Bespin. Draft after draft, Cloud City changed, even though it would still turn out to be a prison for Han, Leia, and Chewie! After various adjustments, it took on its identity as the mining center floating amid pastel clouds that we all have come to know. Of course, the makers of *Star Wars* knew about Cloud City long before we ever did. Ralph McQuarrie had already sketched it out for *A New Hope*, with a drawing entitled "City in Clouds." His idea would later be developed for *The Empire Strikes Back*. Seen from the outside, the floating city almost looks like a giant spaceship, recalling the one seen in another film, *Close Encounters of the Third Kind* (1977), which McQuarrie also worked on. He explains: "You may note it bears a bit of resemblance to the mothership in *Close Encounters*, which I also created. I've painted this scene a number of times already, originally for the first film. I wanted something more mechanical and I came up with something like the side of an aircraft carrier. I put a kind of city on the top of it that looked like it had ancient monuments." The famed Cloud City skyline certainly stands out for the cylindrical towers that McQuarrie himself conceived. He continues, "I came up with round buildings because, if they were square, they'd wind up looking just like the Black Tower at Universal Studios. [...] You try and come up with an idea for a building that hasn't already been done, which is pretty hard to do." McQuarrie also designed the cloud cars, small atmospheric repulsocraft with rounded contours often seen buzzing around Cloud City, which evolved from vehicles initially called "pod cars." All of these elements would be combined using an array of different techniques, since it had been decided not to create a full-blown model of the floating city, but only a handful of buildings it contained—seven, to be exact. Production meeting notes from June 11, 1979 show that in order to bring Cloud City to life, technical efforts would "consist of paintings, cutouts, and foreground 3D pieces."

For these evocative cityscapes, McQuarrie conveyed his ideas for the visuals to production designer Norman Reynolds and the special effects crew, which included Dennis Muren, Ken Ralston, and young Mike Pangrazio, who had come on board in late 1978, just after his 21st birthday. Also on the

01 Cloud City and a twin-pod cloud car in a painting by Ralph McQuarrie.

02 The rebels run towards the *Millennium Falcon* in the dusk, in a painting by Ralph McQuarrie.

03 Early concepts by McQuarrie for Cloud City's architecture and inhabitants.

04

06

04 Model maker Tom Rudduck working on a model of a cloud car. Those ships were first designed by Ralph McQuarrie.

05 Model maker Scott Marshall works on the details of one of the two pilots of a cloud car.

06 Han looks over the city in a brief moment of peace, as painted by McQuarrie.

team was Harrison Ellenshaw, who had created spectacular matte paintings for *A New Hope*. These artists worked together to come up with a host of brilliant sequences. As Dennis Muren points out, the clouds were based on actual clouds: "Here in Cloud City, we're dealing with real backgrounds shot by Brian Johnson from an airplane. So we had light-colored backgrounds with a lot of bluescreen—the same problem they had on *Superman* —and this factor multiplied the difficulties ten-fold. In order to achieve

a high degree of realism, we've gone heavily into diffusion on the spaceships. We've knocked the blacks out of them, we've degraded the image." As for the *Millennium Falcon*, Ken Ralston said in: "We did some tricks where we would do some dissolves so the Falcon would look like it was flying out of clouds. The moving clouds was a nightmare for the optical department." For example, for the shot of the *Millennium Falcon* arriving on Cloud City, a matte painting by Harrison Ellenshaw was combined with footage

taken by the Night Crew of the very heavy *Millennium Falcon* model built for *A New Hope*. To convey the different points of view after the landing, during the exchange between Han and Lando, different matte paintings were used. An establishing shot also resulted from such complex collaboration. For the scene showing Han peering out the window at a cloud car, Mike Pangrazio's matte painting of clouds in the foreground was combined with a matte painting of Cloud City by McQuarrie. To make things even more

07 Lando greets his guests in a painting by McQuarrie. He's accompanied by a woman, an aide that will be later replaced by male cyborg Lobot.

08 Master Ralph McQuarrie working on a matte painting. He's adding the final details to a painting depicting the arrival of the *Millennium Falcon* on Cloud City.

09 Using the PA system, matte photographer Neil Krepela would warn the colleagues at ILM to not shake the building. The matte painting department was on the second floor and even a small vibration would ruin hours of work.

10 The landing on Cloud City was a very difficult scene to film, combining several tecniques. It's one of the greatest achivements of the aptly named "Night Crew."

10

9

complicated, the scenes in Cloud City take place at different times of day, which meant that different backgrounds had to be used, with varying shades of colors. As Ellenshaw tells us, "Typical of George was his very clever concept of showing the passage of time in Cloud City by going from sunrise to daylight, when Luke arrives, to sunset, when the *Millennium Falcon* leaves." A truly titanic endeavor, if one also considers that the special effects people wound up working day and night to meet their deadlines—thus the birth of the legendary *Star Wars* "Night Crew." All that effort still

revolved around what Lucas —and Ralph McQuarrie—had envisioned. "Ralph kept saying to me, 'I don't want to know anything about how things work around here, I just want to paint," recalls Ellenshaw. "And I said, 'Fine, you paint. Any shot you want to start, you do it and let me worry about making it work.'"

In the first draft of *The Empire Strikes Back* script, Lando greets Han and his cohorts in the company of an alien, known as Bahiri. He was supposed to have been the leader of the native populace of Bespin—tall beings with large eyes, devoid

of noses as we know them, and, in keeping with several preliminary sketches done by McQuarrie, having four arms. They would have been creatures much different from the coarse, short Bespinites that would come to be known as the Ugnaughts. Also in the first draft, it was supposed to be the killing of Bahiri at the hands of stormtroopers that convinced Lando to change sides. After a few modifications, that character was transformed into a male human, who, after Lando, would be Cloud City's most notable personage, the loyal and laconic Lobot. Listed

11 Time to relax in Bespin. Leia wears a white and red-brown dress, a present from her host. She has no idea Darth Vader is at the same location...

12 The Cloud City living quarters scene was filmed by Kershner in late April, 1979. The original dialogue between Leia and Han had been revised by the director and the actors many times before shooting.

12

in the closing credits only as "Lando's Aide," he was played by the famed character actor with a penetrating gaze, John Hollis, who had been active in movie and TV roles since the 1960s. Another version of Lando's aide had also been included since the early drafts of the script, and in several production paintings was depicted as a tall woman with a gentle bearing and dark skin.

That character would later be modified to become a cyborg, and Hollis was chosen for the part. His shaved head was fitted with a cybernetic implant prop, complete with batteries that powered its lights—it was heavy and uncomfortable to wear, according to Hollis. At first, he was only scheduled to take part in one week's worth of shooting, but because of the film's extended shooting

schedule he remained a fixture on the set for ten weeks. The name Lobot is short for "Lobotomy," which may give us some clue as to the character's backstory. Up until the fifth draft of the script he had at least one spoken line, but it was decided that he would not speak a word in *The Empire Strikes Back*. Lobot was perfectly able to speak, however, as seen in other storytelling. ☢

13

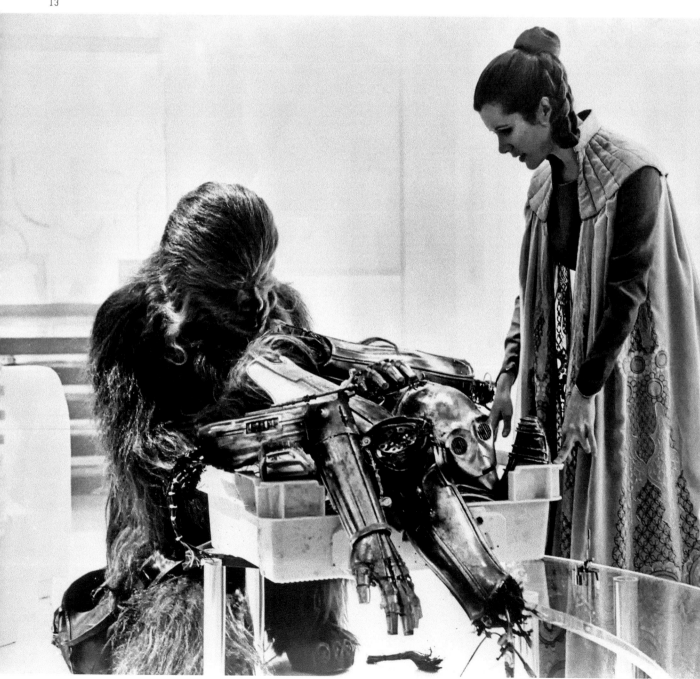

13 A destroyed C-3PO is taken by Chewie to the big panoramic room, interrupting Han and Leia. A moment later, Lando will join them.

14 The mechanics of Bespin, the Ugnaughts, were originally called "Hogmen." In this scene, the prop for assassin droid IG-88, whose only other scene is on the deck of Darth Vader's flagship, was reused and appears behind Chewbacca.

15 Actor John Hollis is Lobot, Lando's aide. The lights on his headpiece were powered by common batteries.

17

16 Carrie Fisher and Peter Mayhew running from Imperial stormtroopers in the corridors of Cloud City.

17 Darth Vader poses with stormtroopers and an Imperial guard on Stage 2. This photo was taken between the scenes filmed on July 6, 1979.

18 After receiving direction from second assistant director Roy Button, Prowse and Ford film the dark and intense torture scene in Cloud City.

18

19

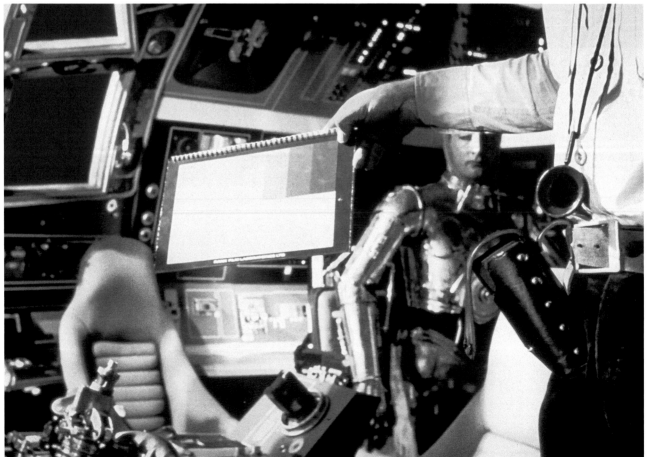

20

21

22

19 White protocol droid K-3PO (left, played by actor Chris Parsons) was manufactured by Cybot Galactica. On Hoth, he had the task of organizing the Echo Base droidpool.

20 Anthony Daniels on the *Millennium Falcon* cockpit set wearing part of his C-3PO costume—which assistant art director Fred Hole and his team worked to make more flexible than it was in the first film.

21 Han Solo puts his hand over C-3PO's mouth during reharsals. In the final shot, Han uses the other hand and wears his Hoth jacket.

22 Actor Anthony Daniels poses with the C-3PO costume. This version had 11 parts and was lighter than the one used in *Star Wars*, which had 20 parts.

23

24

25

23 Special effects artist Brian Johnson and his team built eight new R2-D2 models for *The Empire Strikes Back*. Among these, two were remote controlled, two were used by actor Kenny Baker, one was used for experimentation.

24 Made of fiberglass instead of aluminum, the new R2-D2 models were lighter than the one used in the first film and could be easily lifted, carried, or fired by a pneumatic cannon.

25 Luke Skywalker (Mark Hamill), wearing his rebel flight suit, and R2-D2 on the campsite set up on Dagobah, waiting to meet the legendary Jedi master Yoda.

26 One of the R2-D2 models built for the film could be submerged in water, a necessary feature because of a scene in which the droid is spat out by a bog creature on Dagobah. Part of the scene was shot at the beginning of 1980, in George Lucas' unfinished swimming pool since the original set was not deep enough.

26

ᒲᕮᐯᓰ ᔑᑌᒲ∀ᑎᓰᔑ

"I KNOW"

Right before Han, Leia, C-3PO, and Chewbacca arrive on Cloud City to have the *Millennium Falcon*'s hyperdrive repaired, the Imperials reach the mining colony with a demand. To protect the independence of his facility, and his life, Lando Calrissian has no choice but to give in. Betrayed by his old friend, whom he actually never trusted in the first place, Solo is therefore tortured in order to lure Luke Skywalker into a trap and later frozen in carbonite as a test—because Darth Vader wants to be sure that when it's Luke's turn, he won't be killed. It's the darkest moment for the rebels, but for Leia and Han it's also the most emotional, the culmination of their love story.

HE ORIGIN – As he stated in a 1977 story conference, George Lucas was planning to develop the romantic connection between Leia, Han, and Luke in the sequel to *Star Wars*: "Han would state his position, sulks off. It should be very mature in the way it works. It's not until later that we realize that Leia doesn't love Luke. It has got to be a real triangle with real emotions; at the same time, it has to end up with good will. Luke has gone off to learn the Force and the ongoing story continues with Leia and Han. The Empire continues to chase them. We keep them in a constant danger situation." Looking for a traditional and effective way to set up the relationship between his heroes, Lucas thought about *Gone with the Wind* (1939) and initially visualized Han as Rhett Butler, Leia as Scarlett O'Hara, and Luke as Ashley Wilkes. Taking inspiration from the well-known characters played by Clark Gable and Vivien Leigh, all the drafts focused on the tension between the princess and the smuggler, creating an equally iconic couple. In the second draft, for example, when the two argue about Solo leaving because of his debt with Jabba the Hutt, he

01

02

tells her: "They say I kiss very well. But don't worry, I'm not going to kiss you here—you see, I'm quite selfish about my pleasures and it wouldn't be much fun for me now." The scene remained in the following drafts, but the line was changed to: "Afraid I was going to leave without giving you a goodbye kiss?" To which Leia replies: "I'd just as soon kiss a Wookiee."

In another scene featured in the second draft, Leia and Han exchange their first kiss aboard the *Millennium Falcon*. This scene as well made it to the final script and was shot, but not exactly as planned, due to the director's improvisation on set: in the script, Leia moves away from Solo; in the film, it's C-3PO who interrupts them. "I think he's rather disconcerted

throughout the film that he's not human," said actor Anthony Daniels (C-3PO). "He doesn't quite understand what kissing is because if there's one thing a robot isn't into it's kissing." It's only on Cloud City that the two really express their feelings for each other, but, once again, it was the set that established how this would happen.

01 "Sir, sir! I've isolated the reverse power flux coupling!" C-3PO interrupts the couple in an ad-libbed moment. This was the very first *Empire* scene for Anthony Daniels (C-3PO) and Carrie Fisher (Leia).

02 The first kiss between Leia and Han, aboard the *Millennium Falcon*, shot on March 14, 1979.

THE SET – On June, 18, 1979, Irvin Kershner, the cast, and the rest of the crew were shooting the carbon freezing chamber scene. It wasn't the easiest set to work on. Built inside Stage 4 at the Elstree Studios, England, 12 feet above the ground, it was completely filled with steam, "which made it photographically very impressive, but physically very uncomfortable" as director of photography Peter Suschitzky described it. Besides, dozens of arc lights raised the temperature. Story-wise it was also a tense moment for Princess Leia and Chewbacca who had to watch Han being frozen in carbonite before their eyes. In Kasdan's final draft, after one last kiss, Leia was supposed to say to Han: "I love you. I couldn't tell you before, but it's true." And he was supposed to reply: "Just remember that, 'cause I'll be back." Kershner, though, was not sure about the dialogue and discussed it in detail with Harrison Ford (Han Solo). Helping the director explore Han's personality, Ford came up with a different line: "Yeah, I

03

04

know. Don't worry, I'll be back." Then, as the conversation went on, the actor realized what his character should've said. As we know from a live recording of that day, Ford's exact words were: "If she says, 'I love you,' and I say, 'I know,' it's beautiful and it's acceptable and it's funny." The change worked. As actress Carrie Fisher recalled later, the cast and crew laughed for about 15 minutes watching the dailies. "It works because they actually can make the transition from that laugh into the fact that it is something very sad." ☮

03 An on-set photo of Han and Leia's goodbye kiss.

04 Entering the carbon-freezing chamber, Solo asks Lando: "What's going on... buddy?" in a derogatory way. Lando replies: "You're being put into carbon freeze." These lines were also decided by Kershner and Ford while they were discussing the scene: in the script, Lando didn't say anything, but they felt he had to contribute to the moment somehow, and Williams agreed.

05 Scene number 379, Han Solo put in carbonite, was shot on June 21, 1979, after many rewrites and rehearsals.

06 Han Solo's face frozen in carbonite was modeled on Harrison Ford's actual face, while Alan Harris (who played Bossk) contributed to Han's body. The two parts were later combined to complete the figure.

05

06

07

07 Ford's contribution to scene 379 was essential. As Kershner commented: "Harrison is a very fine actor, I regarded that scene as entirely his, which is why I gave him so much opportunity to tell me how he thought we should treat it."

"*I* AM YOUR FATHER"

After having a vision of Han Solo and Leia in extreme danger, Luke Skywalker decides to leave Dagobah and go save his friends. Yoda succeeds in dissuading him, but not for long, and soon the young apprentice takes off aboard his X-wing, headed for the trap set by Darth Vader. Once Luke reaches Cloud City, he finds himself in front of his worst enemy. The ensuing confrontation is the very first lightsaber duel between the two, as well as the encounter that will forever change the course of their lives. Featuring what is one of the biggest revelations—and most misquoted lines!—in cinema history, the scene sheds light on Luke Skywalker's parentage; however, not many people know that Luke wasn't the only one groping in the dark…

THE SEQUENCE – The duel begins in the carbon-freezing chamber on Cloud City. The dark lord greets the boy reminding him that, despite the Force being strong with him, he has yet to become a Jedi. Luke replies by drawing his lightsaber, thus opening the duel. During the battle, Vader manages to drive Skywalker towards the carbon freezing pit, into which he falls. The attempt to freeze his opponent, however, fails as Yoda's apprentice uses the Force to burst out. Still fighting, Luke and the Sith Lord end up in the reactor shaft, where Vader traps his opponent on a catwalk from which he cannot escape. There, he cuts off Luke's right hand, thus disarming him. Before seemingly swinging his death blow, Darth Vader prompts Skywalker to join the dark side and complete the training under his guidance. Though helpless and severely injured, the boy declines and angrily accuses the Sith Lord of having killed his father. That's when Vader reveals the truth to Luke Skywalker: he is Luke's father (but it isn't until *Return of the Jedi* that the audience learns his true name: Anakin Skywalker). Refusing to believe it and yet sensing that Vader is telling the truth, Luke lets himself fall into the air shaft below him, choosing the void over the dark side.

01

01 The duel between Luke and Darth Vader starts in the smoke-filled chamber where Han had previously been frozen in carbonite. Instead of David Prowse in the Vader costume, there was experienced sword master Bob Anderson who acted opposite Mark Hamill during the scene. During his career, Anderson had also worked alongside legends Errol Flynn and Douglas Fairbanks.

02 The action moves inside the reactor control room set. As stunt coordinator Peter Diamond recalled: "When we were in the reactor room, with pieces of machinery being thrown at the artists, particularly Luke Skywalker, [Mark Hamill] stood a great chance of being seriously injured."

03

03 Luke follows Vader from the carbon-freezing chamber to the reactor control room. "At the time we filmed *Star Wars*," recalled Mark Hamill, "I had no idea Darth Vader was my father, and I don't think Alec Guinness did, either, because in the scene where I ask him who my father was, he hesitated."

THE ORIGIN – During a story conference held from November 28 to December 2, 1977, the identity of Luke Skywalker's father was still a work in progress as George Lucas would constantly revise it in accordance with the plot development. The evolution of Luke's lost sibling was, on the other hand, a much clearer picture. "The idea is that Luke's father had two children who were twins… He took one of them to an uncle on one side of the universe and one to the other side of the universe, so that they would be safe." The plot twist of Darth Vader being Luke's father—so a bad guy and not a hero—was ultimately established in the original second draft handwritten by Lucas; however, such revelation was eventually left out in the typed version as a special measure to avoid plot leaks: "The issue of Luke's father I kept pretty quiet for a long, long time," Lucas would later admit. "I didn't tell anyone… I just couldn't risk it getting out." By necessity, Lucas and Irvin Kershner had to disclose the truth to Mark Hamill, who was however informed only upon shooting the scene: "I met with Mark, and said, 'Uh, you know that Darth Vader's your father.' 'Wha—?'" recalled Kershner. "I told Mark, 'Don't tell anybody—especially don't tell David Prowse,'" further explained Lucas. Despite starring as Darth Vader himself, Prowse was given a misleading line which Hamill would have to ignore. The voice-over for Darth Vader was then handled by James Earl Jones, who recorded his lines—including the paternity revelation—in late 1979/early 1980: "When I first saw the dialogue that said, 'Luke, I am your father,' I said to myself, 'He's lying, I wonder how they're gonna play that lie out.'" On May 20, 1980, the movie premiered at the Odeon in London, revealing the

04 Vader reveals his secret to his son. In a scene that didn't make the final cut, after Luke let himself fall from the gantry, the Sith Lord watches him levitating, raised by the reactor's wind.

05 "The most frightening thing I had to do was to back away from Darth Vader along a plank nine inches wide, 30 feet above the ground, with two wind machines going full-blast," said Hamill.

04

05

06 Luke battles Darth Vader in the carbon freezing chamber in this concept art by Ralph McQuarrie.

07 "Sword fight on antenna" by McQuarrie, concept art painting dated August 21–22, 1978. McQuarrie also realized the matte painting for the Cloud City reactor shaft that would be used to finalize the film sequence.

identity of Luke's father to the world (and Prowse). Predictably, the audience was taken aback by the plot-twist, and consequently started speculating about whether Darth Vader was really the father of Luke Skywalker. Throughout a survey he personally conducted, Kershner found out that "children up to the age of about seven didn't believe that Darth Vader was Luke's father. They think he's lying. Above the age of seven, they accept it—and it sends a chill up their spine." To dispel any doubts, people would need to wait for the third instalment of the saga; for much to learn, as a certain Jedi Master would say, they still had.

08 Vader cuts off Luke's right hand with his lightsaber. The scene would be evoked in *Return of the Jedi* (1983) when Luke cuts off Vader's right hand in front of the Emperor.

09 Scene 400— which included Vader's revelation to Luke—required nearly a week to be completed. Part of it also had to be re-shot because the film was damaged in the laboratory.

10 Whilst filming the 'Cloud City's weather vane' scene, Hamill was hanging 40 feet off the ground, attached to a safety wire.

11 Luke Skywalker clings to a weather vane under Cloud City in this concept art by McQuarrie.

12 Chewbacca and Leia go back to Cloud City to rescue Luke, after Leia senses that he's in danger.

11

12

13

14

15

R.M°QUARRIE

R.M°QUARRIE

13 In this painting by McQuarrie, Leia, R2-D2 and C-3PO watch surgical droid 2-1B treating Luke's wound in the medical bay.

14 A promotion image of the rebel fleet at the end of *Empire*, achieved through a composition of ship miniatures against a starred backdrop.

15 "Luke and Leia (Star Cruiser)" production painting by McQuarrie.

16 Actual frame based on McQuarrie's artwork with the addition of a nebula element—realized with flour, over-exposures, and a mirror.

16

ᒣᔑᔑᑊ ᒐᕔᒣᔑ ᗡ7ᗄᑕᒣ

BACK IN THE THEATERS

The London Symphony Orchestra had once again gathered under the direction of John Williams to record the soundtrack. George Lucas had already put the finishing touches on the opening crawl text. And after the last, harrowing phases of post-production, *The Empire Strikes Back* was ready to hit theaters... for the first time. To this date, after many re-releases, it remains one of the best loved chapters in the entire *Star Wars* saga. But on the eve of the premiere, even its stars had their doubts. At the time, Mark Hamill remarked, "I don't think *Empire* can become a phenomenon. You can't take people by surprise like we did the first time. There's been so much down the pike since we came out. But I think it's going to be a smashing success."

THE DEBUT – But George Lucas kept the faith. Despite all the glitches and delays, on March 13, 1980 he declared, "I think it's a better film than the first one." The finished version was previewed by Lucas on April 19 at the Northpoint Theatre in San Francisco, where *A New Hope* had been previewed three years earlier. Following a sneak peek preview at London's Dominion Theatre, the official world premiere was held at the Kennedy Center Washington, D.C., on May 17, 1980, four days before the release. The Kennedy Center premiere was a benefit screening for the Special Olympics,

with 300 guest athletes in the audience of some 1100. The cast was also in attendance, except for Anthony "C-3PO" Daniels, who called in sick. On May 20, the entire cast would gather in London for the Royal Charity premiere. Backstage, Princess Leia was photographed with a real princess, Margaret. Then on May 21, *The Empire Strikes Back* at long last made its official theatrical debut. Initially, 70mm copies were sent out to 127 movie theatres throughout the United States, prior to capillary distribution of the 35mm version. Theatres sold out quickly and were forced to change their scheduling to accommodate the crowds. In Los Angeles, the Egyptian Theatre began showing *The*

Empire Strikes Back at midnight on May 21, with screenings around the clock for an entire day, practically non-stop. Long lines stretched in front of theaters across the country, with many fans dressed as their favorite *Star Wars* characters—a trend that became popular with the release of the saga's first sequel. Magazine covers, radio and television interviews, and the enthusiasm of fans paved the way for phase two: Thanks to the distribution of 35mm copies beginning June 18, *The Empire Strikes Back* would be shown in some 1400 theatres by the end of summer.

Another glitch, however, lay just around the corner. George Lucas attended a screening to check the audience's reaction.

01 The "Style A" poster for *The Empire Strike Back*, by Roger Kastel, is inspired by *Gone With the Wind*.

He noted that people were somewhat bewildered by the ending, and concluded that the film needed three new shots added. Joe Johnson and his crew were alerted, and as quickly as possible—about three weeks—they satisfied Lucas's request. ILM's Tom Smith explains: "The new work required building a couple of quick models and recycling stock shots for the smaller moving spaceships. The work was all done in record time thanks to the recycled shots." In the end, Lucas was pleased with the results, even though he reportedly congratulated Johnson's team with a bit of wry sarcasm: "Wait a minute. If you guys did this so fast, why did it take so long to do all the other ones?"

Despite the mixed reviews by critics early on, *The Empire Strikes Back* would soon go on to achieve both critical acclaim and huge commercial success. Floored by the film's darker tones, people appreciated its artistic quality, its knack for keeping suspense levels high, its dexterous use of cliffhangers and its sheer inventiveness. Today *The Empire Strikes Back* is considered a major work of the science-fiction genre, and in 2010 it was selected by the United States Library of Congress to be included in the National Film Registry, a sign of the film's artistic and cultural value. In terms of money-making, *The Empire Strikes Back* proved that such a colossal blockbuster was possible even without investments from the major film studios. George Lucas' dream had come to life, and his outrageous gamble had paid off. In just three months he'd broken even. Lucasfilm was a creative community able to go head-to-head with the major studios and win—while maintaining complete control of production, financing, rights, and deals. The special-effects house Industrial Light & Magic would go on to fully exploit the avant-garde experimental work Lucas had ordered and put that knowledge and those skills to work on other projects. As far as *Star Wars* fans were concerned, lots of questions came cropping up: Was Luke really Darth Vader's son? Who was "the other" that Yoda spoke of? Who was hiding beneath the hood of the Emperor? What would become of Han Solo? Those questions would be answered three years later in *Return of the Jedi...* and in the continuing chapters. All *Star Wars* lovers needed was a little patience! ☙

02 Style "B" poster for the U.S. official release. Art by Tom Jung.

03 Sketch by Roger Kastel for the "Style A" poster. It includes assassin droid IG-88 instead of Boba Fett.

04 This sketch of the Kastel "Style A" poster includes Boba Fett.

05 Sketch by Tom Jung for the "Style B" poster, focusing on Vader.

06 Poster by Lawrence Noble for the 10th Anniversary of Empire.

STAR WARS LIBRARY

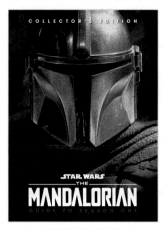

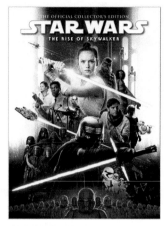

THE MANDALORIAN:
GUIDE TO SEASON ONE

THE MANDALORIAN
THE ART AND IMAGERY
VOLUME 2

STAR WARS: THE RISE OF SKYWALKER:
THE OFFICIAL COLLECTOR'S EDITION

STAR WARS: THE SKYWALKER SAGA
THE OFFICIAL COLLECTOR'S EDITION

- *ROGUE ONE: A STAR WARS STORY*
  THE OFFICIAL COLLECTOR'S EDITION
- *ROGUE ONE: A STAR WARS STORY*
  THE OFFICIAL MISSION DEBRIEF
- *STAR WARS: THE LAST JEDI* THE OFFICIAL
  COLLECTOR'S EDITION
- *STAR WARS: THE LAST JEDI* THE OFFICIAL
  MOVIE COMPANION
- *STAR WARS: THE LAST JEDI*
  THE ULTIMATE GUIDE

- *SOLO: A STAR WARS STORY*
  THE OFFICIAL COLLECTOR'S EDITION
- *SOLO: A STAR WARS STORY* THE
  ULTIMATE GUIDE
- **THE BEST OF *STAR WARS INSIDER*** VOLUME 1
- **THE BEST OF *STAR WARS INSIDER*** VOLUME 2
- **THE BEST OF *STAR WARS INSIDER*** VOLUME 3
- **THE BEST OF *STAR WARS INSIDER*** VOLUME 4
- *STAR WARS:* LORDS OF THE SITH
- *STAR WARS:* HEROES OF THE FORCE

- *STAR WARS:* ICONS OF THE GALAXY
- *STAR WARS:* THE SAGA BEGINS
- *STAR WARS* THE ORIGINAL TRILOGY
- *STAR WARS:* ROGUES, SCOUNDRELS
  AND BOUNTY HUNTERS
- *STAR WARS* CREATURES, ALIENS,AND DROIDS
- *STAR WARS: THE RISE OF SKYWALKER* THE
  OFFICIAL COLLECTOR'S EDITION
- *THE MANDALORIAN* THE ART AND IMAGERY
  VOLUME 1

- *THE MANDALORIAN* THE ART AND IMAGERY
  VOLUME 2
- *STAR WARS: THE EMPIRE STRIKES BACK*
  THE 40TH ANNIVERSARY COLLCTORS'
  EDITION
- *STAR WARS: AGE OF RESISTANCE*
  THE OFFICIAL COLLCTORS' EDITION
- *STAR WARS: THE SKYWALKER SAGA*
  THE OFFICIAL COLLECTOR'S EDITION
- *THE MANDALORIAN* GUIDE TO SEASON ONE

MARVEL LIBRARY

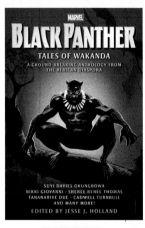

BLACK PANTHER
TALES OF WAKANDA

**MARVEL STUDIOS' THE COMPLETE
AVENGERS**

MARVEL STUDIOS' BLACK WIDOW

MARVEL: THE FIRST 80 YEARS

MARVEL CLASSIC NOVELS
- **WOLVERINE** WEAPON X OMNIBUS
- **SPIDER-MAN** THE DARKEST HOURS OMNIBUS
- **SPIDER-MAN** THE VENOM FACTOR OMNIBUS
- **X-MEN AND THE AVENGERS**
  GAMMA QUEST OMNIBUS
- **X-MEN** MUTANT FACTOR OMNIBUS

NOVELS
- **SPIDER-MAN MILES MORALES** WINGS OF FURY
- **MORBIUS** THE LIVING VAMPIRE: BLOOD TIES
- **ANT-MAN** NATURAL ENEMY
- **AVENGERS** EVERYBODY WANTS TO RULE
  THE WORLD
- **AVENGERS** INFINITY
- **BLACK PANTHER** WHO IS THE BLACK PANTHER?

- **CAPTAIN AMERICA** DARK DESIGNS
- **CAPTAIN MARVEL** LIBERATION RUN
- **CIVIL WAR**
- **DEADPOOL** PAWS
- **SPIDER-MAN** FOREVER YOUNG
- **SPIDER-MAN** KRAVEN'S LAST HUNT
- **THANOS** DEATH SENTENCE
- **VENOM** LETHAL PROTECTOR
- **X-MEN** DAYS OF FUTURE PAST
- **X-MEN** THE DARK PHOENIX SAGA
- **SPIDER-MAN** HOSTILE TAKEOVER

ART BOOKS
- **MARVEL'S *SPIDER-MAN MILES MORALES***
  THE ART OF THE GAME
- **MARVEL'S *AVENGERS*** THE ART OF THE GAME

- **MARVEL'S *SPIDER-MAN*** THE ART OF THE GAME
- **MARVEL *CONTEST OF CHAMPIONS***
  THE ART OF THE BATTLEREALM
- *SPIDER-MAN: INTO THE SPIDER-VERSE:*
  THE ART OF THE MOVIE
- **THE ART OF IRON MAN**
  10TH ANNIVERSARY EDITION

MOVIE SPECIALS
- **MARVEL STUDIOS' *SPIDER-MAN FAR
  FROM HOME***
- **MARVEL STUDIOS' *ANT MAN & THE WASP***
- **MARVEL STUDIOS' *AVENGERS: ENDGAME***
- **MARVEL STUDIOS' *AVENGERS: INFINITY WAR***
- **MARVEL STUDIOS' *BLACK PANTHER*
  (COMPANION)**

- **MARVEL STUDIOS' *BLACK WIDOW***
- **MARVEL STUDIOS' *CAPTAIN MARVEL***
- **MARVEL STUDIOS' *SPIDER-MAN: FAR
  FROM HOME***
- **MARVEL STUDIOS: THE FIRST TEN YEARS**
- **MARVEL STUDIOS' *THOR: RAGNAROK***

- *SPIDER-MAN: INTO THE SPIDER-VERSE*

AVAILABLE AT ALL GOOD BOOKSTORES AND ONLINE

TITAN-COMICS.COM | **TITAN**BOOKS.COM